Life

Be

Crazy

Also by Roni Blanche:

*Life Gone South (when I ran away
to live at the beach and be a writer)*
A Memoir

Life Is A Beach – After I'm Gone
A Novel

Life Be Crazy

(so why should I be sane?!)

Roni Blanche

ISBN: 0692719008
ISBN-13: 978-0692719008

CONTENTS

Introduction   1

I love you, I love you not   2

Who The Hell Am I?   12

Kiss Carrie Bradshaw Good-bye   26

The Craziest One Of All   40

Get Off My Face   52

No thanks, I'll pass   64

Tit for Tat   80

Why Didn't My Mother Have Me Tested?   94

"O" My   114

Rebel Holler   128

The Final Countdown   158

Acknowledgments   169

INTRODUCTION

Life be crazy, Folks.

It always is, it always will be.

So there is only one thing to do:

"Let's go crazy

let's get nuts

let's look 4 the purple banana

'til they put us in the truck,

let's go!"

Prince Rogers Nelson

(1958 - 2016)

I love you,
I love you not

(Fall 2013)

I love you, I love you not

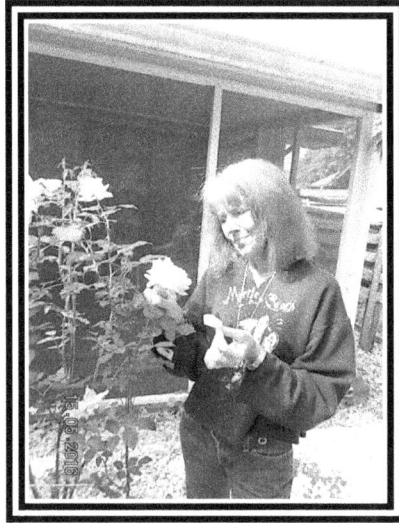

(Braving evil allergens, prickly thorns, and buzzing bees in our
rose garden to decide: Do I love you, do I love you not?)

Our relationship has been rocky lately. I'm not sure I
can go on with it. We used to have good times, lots of
good times in fact, and it felt easy and comfortable
being together. Now I feel mostly pain and
disappointment; the ease is gone. There is still some
love here – we've been together too long and shared too
much for my love to have died completely – but I think
I'm going to have to break up. I'm tired of hurting. I just
don't know how to end it without causing more hurt.

3

No, I'm not talking about splitting up with my life buddy DMan. He's sweet as pecan pie with a dollop of Cool Whip and as rock-steady a boyfriend as the Chevy Trailblazer he drives. DMan is definitely not the problem. My body is the problem; she keeps letting me down.

Take the past several months for instance – please, I'm begging you, take them, they've been miserable – and see how she has treated me. First, she allows a perky little yellow flower like ragweed to attack me, causing bucketfuls of snot to collect in my head, trickle like acid down my throat, and congeal into globs of ghastly green which my chest chooses to upchuck day and night. This phlegm fiesta ritual goes on from mid-August until late October every year. No wonder I hate fall.

In the meantime, through all of this allergic blowing and hacking, I started a fabulous new job. But does Ms. Body have my back and support me in my new challenge like a good partner should? Oh yeah, she has my back all right, bent over like a crone and in excruciating pain. Seems she doesn't believe the agony of allergies is enough, so she gives in to an especially explosive cough and lets my low back go out. Nice. Now I not only look older than most of my stylish stylist coworkers (my new job is a Client Services Coordinator at an upscale-ish salon), but I am hobbling around like I need a walker for support and can't do a simple task like bend over to unload towels from the dryer, which we do all day long, without groaning and grimacing. The staff probably thinks I am supplementing my Social Security check with the salon job. This is so not the I-may-be-older-but-I'm-still-hip impression I wanted to make.

Finally, I caught a couple of breaks. A hard frost croaked the ragweed, and my allergies subsided. An awesome chiropractor – and $150 worth of office visits I couldn't afford – got my low back unlocked. But just when I was starting to believe my body and I had made a truce, WHAM: the bitch pimps me out to the common cold. For two weeks now, sleep – when I'm not being jolted awake by coughing, that is – has been my only solace, nestled between fuzzy-headed mornings and chartreuse-colored snot-filled days. Even the simplest efforts wear me slick, and by evening I hurt all over and barely have the energy to eat. I can't taste anything anyway. Some truce.

I am not a lousy partner either. Ms. Body cannot say that I neglect her. We eat vegetarian – which isn't easy when you live smack dab in the crosshairs of cattle country and poultry farm paradise – as much as possible. We stretch every morning to stay flexible, work out every evening for her cardio health and strength. There is a vintage hat box on my kitchen counter full of pills that I spend a fortune on in order to optimize Ms. Body's well-being: Biotin to make her hair and nails grow and shine; Hyaluronic acid to support her saggy skin; fish oil and low-dose aspirin for a happy heart and less inflammation; hormones to halt the hot flashes, mitigate the mood swings of menopause, and help her still want to sex it up with DMan; Flonase plus a pharmacy aisle of OTC allergy meds to help her fight off that pesky pollen; Kava to calm her ever-present anxiety; and multi-vitamins to take care of anything the other drugs don't do. I hate taking pills, yet I take so many I'm surprised they aren't shooting out of every orifice. But I do it, I choke them down daily, all for her benefit.

And how does she repay me for all the TLC I lavish on her? With betrayal and pain, that's how! She betrays me by allowing all manner of fucuckta foreign bodies into our relationship to wreak havoc on our happy homeostasis and create an ongoing orgy of sickness. The worst betrayal, though, is when Ms. Body lets me down and I cannot do the things I used to do. Work out for an hour in a Zumba class? Three years ago, no problem. Not anymore. After ten minutes I'm drenched in sweat, at 20 minutes I'm gasping for air and can barely lift my arms to do Jazz hands, by halfway through the class I have completely overheated and am hacking up a lung, which brings on a surprise tinkle and I am done. Zumba . . . denied. What about heading out for an evening of cocktails and dancing after working all day? Um, no again. Just having the energy to make it to nine o'clock on a work night is a miracle. My party days are definitely over.

But the pain isn't over. Oh no, Ms. Body is the Queen of Pain. Pain in my feet, even though I eschew sexy stilettos à la Carrie Bradshaw – my favorite fashion idol – and opt for spongy-soled, clunky clogs to pamper her little piggies. Pain in my knees, no matter how much mentholated muscle rub I slather on them. To varying degrees and not always at the same time, I suffer throbbing pain in my thumbs, shooting pain in my shoulders, and lingering pain in my low back. The Queen provides a plethora of pain for my amuse(abuse)ment.

As any good couples counselor would tell us, I am at fault too. I admit it. Smoking has always been my vice of choice, which, I know, does NOT do a body good. I've tried breaking up with that habit many times but couldn't live without my beloved smokes for long. I also drink, but generally just one glass of red wine a night (okay, one BIG glass!) to ease the day's aches. Taking things too seriously is another bad habit I can't shake, which I'm sure stresses Ms. Body out more than is good for her. So I'm not the perfect partner – is that sufficient reason for her to make my life miserable?

I shouldn't complain; there are many people out there with many more pains and problems than I have. And to be fair – and ease the sting of all my bitching so she doesn't bring on shingles or amebic dysentery in retribution – Ms. Body hasn't let me down totally. She keeps breathing all day, every day, despite my incessant smoking. Thanks for that, Girlfriend! She digests all that I put into her, including an entire can of Stax Salt & Vinegar chips that I've been known to mindlessly munch until my tongue is stinging and raw, with her rarely revolting by giving me heartburn or diarrhea. She takes me where I need to go, with minimal mishaps and no support equipment required. Yet. My mama has become the bionic woman over the years, with artificial knees and hips installed, so if Ms. Body gives in to genetics then I'm sure I'm headed for joint replacement or a Jazzy scooter. Or both.

Okay, so maybe Ms. Body isn't the most horrible partner in the world and I'm being too hard on her for letting me down. Perhaps I am the horrible one for being such a fair-weather lover. My pattern has always been that when things are going smooth with "us" in any of my relationships, I am my partner's biggest fan and cheerleader. But if they disappoint me or cause me pain, when I've had enough, I will send them packing to Bye-byeville and forget their name before they arrive. That's just me.

It sounds mean, I know, but these things happen all the time. A couple that has been together 50, sometimes even 60, seemingly happy years all of a sudden has had their fill and splits up. No big deal. Life goes on. Yeah, I can be a heartless bitch, but growing old together can be a bitch as well. And that's one too many bitches in this relationship for my taste.

So it's come to that time for us, Ms. Body. I've had enough. I'm cutting you loose and wishing you well on your solo journey. Maybe you'll find someone out there much better for you, some tea-totalling, non-smoker with a more positive attitude and less bat-crap crazy. Maybe there is some "body" out there for me too. I'm thinking a Yorkie dog would be a good fit: silky hair, I wouldn't have to shave my legs, and they are bitchy by nature yet people still love them. Or Cher. Then I could have any kind of hair I wanted on any given day, pay someone to shave my legs, have enough money to fix anything that ached and lift anything that sagged, and being a bitch is practically required to be a diva. Definitely Cher.

Who The Hell

Am I?

(Summer 2013)

(Sister K and I crashed a holiday party in December 2014.
She's the one in the wicked cool hat!)

My sister K and I were hanging out the other day, and out of the blue she says, "I don't know who I am anymore. I don't fit in anywhere. I'm not young, but I'm not old either. So who the hell am I?"

My first thought was "Is menopause bitch-slapping her too?" because that hormone-robbing hag (menopause, not my sister!) had been smacking me around pretty hard lately. But the more we talked, the more I understood that her quandary had nothing to do with menopause and realized I felt exactly the same way: Middle age is no (wo)man's land. Halfway between birth and death (we hope), being in our 40s and 50s is confusing. And frustrating. We literally are not young anymore, nor are we old (except that we seem old to those that *are* young).

When we were young, things were much simpler. Being young meant having big fun and little responsibility, like working part-time slinging burgers at the Tastee-Freez and then hanging out with friends at the drive-in movie, singing "We go together like rama lama lama ka dinga da dinga dong" at the top of our lungs while watching *Grease* for the gozillionth time, and forgetting what piddly worries we might have by topping off our Big Gulp drink with Everclear or taking a hit off a passed-around joint. (Just don't mix the two unless you want to end up buzzed off your butt in the backseat of your date's car, take my word on this!) It meant cruising in the nearest big town to check out cute boys and blasting your newest Loverboy cassette tape. With gas at only 79 cents per gallon back then, driving up and down Kearney Street – the preferred cruising spot in the "metropolis" of Springfield near where I lived – all night long was cheap entertainment.

We young'uns wore bell-bottom Levis and feathered hair, drove Pintos or Vegas or VW Bugs, parked on country roads to make out with our sweeties, then snuck in past curfew with hickeys that we tried to pass off as curling iron burns the next morning when our parents asked, "What the hell is that?"

We knew we weren't old because *old folks* had bursitis and mortgages, smoked pipes and cigars and drank instant coffee, and went to church socials or PTA meetings for "fun." Oldsters wore polyester pants, knee-high hose that bagged at the ankles, and spongy-soled shoes. The aging ladies got perms or a weekly wash-and-set at the beauty parlor, the geriatric gentlemen drove around town in tank-like Buicks and Plymouths, and the closest those two got to making out was a good-night peck on the cheek. Some of those old people may have even been *in* their 40s, but they seemed ancient to us. It was simple then: when you got to be a certain age, you dressed and acted "your age."

But no more. If you could meet Sister K, headed toward the far side of 40 herself, you would see she is the antithesis of old: dark chocolate hair swinging in a CHI-sleeked "Rachel" 'do, body-hugging shirts and sequin-pocketed jeans showing off her curvaceous-ness, with a mishmash of Christian and biker chick tattoos decorating her arms and legs. She rode a Harley until it finally went kaput and says "wicked cool" about everything. No way could she be described as old.

In outward appearance, I'm definitely not as wicked cool as she, but I'm still wearing low-rider jeans without sporting a belly-flopping hangover or plumber's crack. The funky cap-toe sneakers and peace sign earrings that I sport as my "signature look" give me a youthful flair. And the only polyester pants that have EVER been on these thighs were part of the Kentucky Fried Chicken uniform I wore to work during my college days. Those pants were mandatory, and I hate, hate, hated them.

Okay, so our look is still in the young(ish) realm. Cool. What about our actions?

Sister K has teenage boys, which brings with it the requisite mommy baggage, but that's not all she's about. Besides making a living driving a school bus like an expert truck rodeoer – I'll bet she is the sexiest bus driver those adolescent boys ever had and provides fodder for many of their under-the-sheet fantasies – she is a faux painting diva, wine blend connoisseur, disco dancer extraordinaire, and super seamstress. She creates and wears these diaphanous ponchos, blinged out with sparkles and feathery trim, that can turn the most blah outfit into party-ware. She also saved my favorite Gap jeans from ending up in the trash by adding zazzy flame patches to the threadbare knees. I get more compliments on those ancient jeans than anything else in my closet. The woman can do it all, and she does. The Energizer Bunny on steroids couldn't keep up with her. She is definitely not living the oldster life.

Me? I'm not so talented or creative, but I try. I try *everything* to try and find that one thing that's going to be "my thing." Here's the "I-tried" short list: playing guitar, harmonica, keyboard and bongos (I swear I've got the music in me, I just can't make it come out); working as a massage therapist (a real one, not a quasi-hooker "masseuse"); being a beach babe (loved it but couldn't afford it forever); and skateboarding. I still have my pin-tail longboard I call Pinkie and she's gorgeous, with hot pink wheels and her underside decorated with groovy stickers like "I'm not perfect, but parts of me are incredible." (DMan bought that sticker for me, so I couldn't NOT use it, right?!) I mostly look at Pinkie these days, spending my spare time writing instead of boarding. But I *could* ride her if I got the urge (and got health insurance, definitely health insurance just in case). And I don't spend all day discussing my aches and pains and surgeries, planning my next meal at the senior-discount buffet, or knitting afghans for gifts that will be hidden in a closet until I come for a visit.

So we don't look old, at least fashion-wise. And we don't act old. Then why the hell can't we figure out who the hell we are?

As I pondered this, I remembered my grandma Helen saying to me, "Honey, I don't feel old. My body may be falling apart and I may look old, but I don't feel it, not inside anyway." *Bazinga!* Grandma was one wise woman. I realized I don't feel old, at least not on the inside. My body sure feels 49 Part Two (I cannot admit to being 50, not yet, so I'm doing 49 again!), some days more like 69 Part Two, but my inside feels like I am 24, tops.

Sister K had her own bazinga moment when I asked her how old she felt: "That's it! My body may feel like I'm in my late 30s, but my spirit is still 21. I think like a kid, that's why I'm more comfortable around kids than people my own age. I've got the wisdom of an older person with a young spirit."

That's true for me as well. While I don't "do" little kids – never had any, never wanted any, and no, I don't babysit no matter how cute you say the little devil is – I feel simpatico hanging with 20-somethings way more than oldsters. I try not to be an old-age bigot, but I have a phobia about visiting senior citizen habitats ever since my 45th birthday. My parents, bless their well-meaning hearts, got sick of me bitching about getting older and surprised me with a birthday lunch at the Senior Center to experience what being old was really like. The Senior Center! The place where everyone had blue hair or no hair at all, the hot topic around the table was who had what removed, and the drill sergeant-type center director spent ten minutes lecturing the lunchers on the proper protocol for the new self-serve salad bar as if they were idiots. Needless to say, I don't mention aging around my parents anymore. Or let them take me out for my birthday.

To get a broader view, I asked others the "How old do you feel outside versus inside?" question, and it seems almost universal that the disparity between body age and spirit age keeps our minds totally befuzzled. Most people reported feeling younger in spirit than body, and the older the person, the wider the gap between the two.

Some examples:

	Body feels	Spirit feels	Age
Roberta	60ish	23/24	50s
Mikey	50	30	50s
Deb	45	23	50s
Eli	35	20	20s

(Actual ages are approximate – I'm not out to "out" anyone's age.)

I wanted to better understand the disparity and the reason behind it, so I asked my sweetie DMan for his opinion. He said, "I guess I feel under 40 all over. If I tried to do things I did when I was 30, I'd probably feel older. But I don't try to do those things anymore." And DMan is older than I am. I do love him to death, but sometimes I just want to wring his neck to choke off his Pollyanna attitude that makes me feel like his "old" lady. Plus, his answer didn't help my understanding one bit.

Then I tried asking Mama and Daddy to tell me their "body versus spirit ages" opinion to use for something I was writing. Big mistake. All I got was righteous rantings as if they were having their 15 minutes of fame on *Oprah*. In a nutshell, Mama's version was "Wake up every day with a sunny outlook and you'll feel your best no matter what age you are," and Daddy spouted off on "I've worked hard all my life and I damn well deserve to feel how old I feel" until I finally gave up. Spoken with good intentions on their part, I'm sure, but no help at all to me.

Looks like I'm on my own to explain the "Who am I?" disconnect. Could it be that our bodies keep on aging but our spirits hold at some prime time when we were at our peak? That's how my memory seems to work. It must have peaked in the 1970s because I can sing every dadblame word of the *Green Acres* theme song but can't remember when I last changed my sheets. (See, that song is playing in my head right now: "Green Acres is the place to be, farm living is the life for me . . . ." The sheets? I don't have a clue how long they've been on the bed. Guess it's time for the sniff test. Or to start writing it on the calendar along with everything else I need to remember.)

If the spirit-peak supposition is true, then maybe what we see as middle-age crazy isn't crazy at all. That paunchy, balding man with the newly-implanted hair plugs who blew his retirement savings on a convertible to impress some bimbo is only acting his spirit age, which locked in as a testosterone-fueled teenager with the hots for topless Corvettes and boobalicious 22-year old blondes. And maybe a lot of oldsters diagnosed with senility are perfectly fine. Their spirits just choose to hang out at the age when having a teddy bear as their lunch companion and calling everyone "Mama" feels right. Life was much nicer with a cuddly friend and Mama around all the time, wasn't it?

Or could it be that the way we feel inside reflects our true soul age, in cosmic terms? What if there is no arrested spirit development involved? What if no matter how old we get to be or how many times our soul gets to hang out in bodily form (If you believe in that sort of thing, which I do, but don't tell my mama. She'll think I'm going straight to hell!), we'll forever stay at our unique and perfect soul age?

That sounds right to me, and my uncle Jesse is a prime example of why. He's on the express train to turning 87 and lives in a nursing home due to Parkinson's disease and the residual effects of several mild strokes, yet his soul is forever youthful. Those honey brown eyes of his exude orneriness. He may not be able to get a forkful of peas to his mouth without spilling half, but he is still the biggest flirt I've ever known. And the best. He's got every female in the facility wrapped around his little finger, and they love it.

He wise cracks. He plays practical jokes. His soul isn't a day over 25. Never has been. Never will be. And it fits him perfectly.

Now I understand why most folks I talked to *feel* like they are in their 20s or 30s on the inside no matter what their birthdate says. If all souls were kid souls, the world would be one giant messy playground and nothing would get accomplished without bribes of milk and cookies. If oldster souls dominated, the world would be nothing but a global AARP convention of oh-my-aching-whatever woes and remember-when-life-was-better bitchfests. At least our 20- or 30-something souls still have hope enough to believe we can make the world better, the energy to keep plugging away until we do, and the smarts to have some fun along the way.

So, who the hell am I? After careful consideration, I've decided that I am a 24-year old soul making the best of life in a 49 Part Two-year old body. Let's see, what was my life like at 24? I was a newly-single gal, after the breakup of my first marriage, with my very own place and a decent paying job. When I wasn't working hard or sleeping soundly, I was boogieing with my sisters every chance I got, wearing jean miniskirts and fringy short boots, drinking cheap beer by the pitcher, and partying with good friends hearty and often.

Being 24 forever? I can live with that.

Kiss

Carrie Bradshaw

Good-bye

(Winter 2012)

(I am a *Sex And The City* devotee –
can you tell?!)

I love, love, love Carrie Bradshaw! Surely you know her, from *Sex And The City*? Played by the effervescently fabulous actress and fashion diva Sarah Jessica Parker? No?? Honey, how big of a rock have you been hiding under?

I will admit: I came to the SATC party late. The series ran from 1998 to 2004, and I never watched it. Never. I was vaguely aware of it from all the Emmys it won, but in my mind it was some smutty show about over-sexed bimbos. It was on HBO, for Pete's sake, and you had to pay to watch that channel like pay-per-view porn. My bestie had mentioned the show from time to time, said what a hoot "the girls" were, and I had enjoyed Sarah Jessica's free-spirited movie characters in *Footloose* and *L.A. Story*, but I had never bothered to give *Sex* a try.

Then one day in 2009, when my entire world was in the crapper and videos were my escape haven, I saw *Sex And The City – The Movie* on the library shelf. It was free, I didn't find anything else I wanted to watch, so I checked it out. I watched it. More accurately, I devoured it. Knowing next to nothing about the characters or back story, I was still hooked. Even by Mr. Big, who hurt my gal Carrie when he couldn't get out of the car to marry her but redeemed himself in the end. In the closet. With double doors. I'll say no more, don't want to be a spoiler, except that seeing that movie was a life changer. I had something to live for again. I had six whole seasons of Carrie Bradshaw's life to catch up on.

Carrie Bradshaw. How do I love her and want to *be* her? Let me count the ways.

#1 WORK: A writer for the fictional newspaper *The New York Star*, Carrie has a weekly column called "Sex And The City" about traversing the trials of relationships and finding love as a single gal in New York City. All that traversing takes her to the coolest NYC hot spots – clubs, restaurants, art gallery openings, benefits, fashion shows – in sky-high stilettos to cavort with celebs and fashionistas and all kinds of quirky characters. Fabulous! (In case you think I don't know any other words besides "fabulous," I do. But when it comes to all things CB and SATC, no other word will do. Watch her. Watch it. You'll see.)

I'm a writer. I could totally do that. I don't know much about sex and I'm certainly no whiz at relationships, but then Carrie doesn't have it all figured out either. That's why her signature phrase "I couldn't help but wonder . . ." starts the last sentence of nearly every column she writes. So, I'm willing to learn right along with her.

#2 LOVE/LUST: Carrie has an on-again, off-again steamy romance with **Big** – a man with money who likes the finer things in life and abso-fucking-lutely will not be corralled by convention – played by hubba-hubba Chris

Noth. Count me in big time! He is the buff bad boy you can't help falling for that makes falling, even when it hurts, so damn much fun. I have played some of Big and Carrie's sizzling scenes over and over so much that my DVD player actually groans when I hit rewind yet again. (In case you are wondering, the "Easy Come, Easy Go" episode is my favorite sizzler. The elevator scene? Oh yeah, it gets my "southern parts" tingling every time!)

As if Big wasn't big enough to make me want her love life (he is!), through the seasons Carrie also hooked up with:

Seth, in a cameo role by Jon Bon Jovi (who just keeps getting hotter with age – so not fair). Carrie meets him in the waiting room when she tries therapy because the girls think she picks the wrong men. She finds out, *after* they have mind-blowing sex unfortunately, that Seth is also Mr. Wrong: he is in therapy because he completely loses interest in a woman after sleeping with her. So long, Seth, but Jon Bon Jovi, you are welcome in my bed anytime. (Season Two)

Aidan Shaw, made irresistibly adorable by John Corbett, a long-time crush of mine since *Northern Exposure* and *My Big Fat Greek Wedding*. Aidan, a laid-back furniture designer, is the antithesis of Big: sweet, open about his feelings, and not afraid of commitment. All of which scares Carrie back into the arms (and Stanhope Hotel bed, from the "Easy" episode where my DVD player groaned the loudest!) of Big. Carrie and Aidan break up in Season Three, reunite and get engaged in Season Four, then split for good before the season ends because he wants to run off and tie the knot and she feels tied in knots because she's not sure she is the marrying type.

Aidan is lovable, has a dog named Pete (I love dogs!), and can make me a big comfy armchair like the one Carrie cozies into for cocktail sipping and *Vogue* reading. So if Carrie can handle Aidan calling her "Pop Tart" and eating fried chicken in her bed for a season or two, then I can too.

Jack Berger (Ron Livingston) is a novelist Carrie meets through her publisher after her columns are turned into a book. They are a perfect intellectual match, effortlessly exchanging razor sharp banter, but can't match up in the sack until they try bringing their banter to bed. Once the sex gets good, the relationship goes bad because Berger can't handle Carrie's authorial success and ends it on a Post-it note. Yeah, a writer breaks up on a Post-it note: "I'm Sorry, I Can't, Don't

Hate Me." Cruel, curt *and* clever, huh?

Even though Berger turns out to be a jerk and isn't my type physically – too hairy, no five o'clock shadow at breakfast for me, thanks – I could go for a guy who stimulates my mind as much as the rest of me. And he rides a motorcycle, even more stimulation for the rest of me. So CB, I'm on board (and definitely won't be bored) with Berger as well. (Seasons Five and Six)

Aleksandr Petrovsky, Carrie's final season final fling, is portrayed by the sexy, sophisticated, and suave Mikhail Baryshnikov. Or Misha, as I affectionately call him ever since I got acquainted with his ballet brilliance and beautiful body in my college Intro to Dance class and came away wet every time (and I don't mean with sweat!). While gallery hopping with Charlotte, Carrie meets Alek, an internationally-renowned Russian "light installation" artist. He romances her old-world style, including a snowy sleigh ride through Central Park and a black-tie slow dance at McDonald's, and convinces Carrie to move to Paris with him for his art show.

Even though Petrovsky doesn't turn out to be the "ridiculous, inconvenient, consuming, can't-live-without-each-other" real love Carrie is looking for, he can light me up anytime. At being romanced by Alek/Misha, I say,

"Da!" (Russion for "yes," in case you didn't know. I googled it.) At being whisked away to an expensive suite in a lovely hotel in Paris by a worldly, wealthy artist that I would do in a New York minute, I say, "Oui!" and "Ooh la la!"

#3 FASHION: Dressed by the ever-quirky and outrageously fashion-forward costume designer/stylist Patricia Field, Carrie Bradshaw shot SATC style into the mainstream of the new millennium even bigger than the show Dallas did in the 1980s. Looking perfectly put together for anything and flawlessly fabulous in everything – from a trench coat over Dolce & Gabbana sequined panties on the runway, to a straight-out-of-Vogue Oscar de la Renta gown at the Metropolitan Opera (and later McDonald's), to deep-cuffed skinny jeans over Manolos running for a taxi – CB pulled viewers in every week to indulge in the fashion as much as the storyline. Bras became chic accessories, instead of just underwear, because she let them show from underneath revealing couture. Single-handedly, Carrie brought Candies back to life and put Manolo Blahniks and Christian Louboutins on every fashionista's wish list.

Please, oh please, if there are any miracles left in

this world, let Pat Field become my fairy godmother and bring me the style savvy and entire wardrobe of Carrie Bradshaw! (But size it up, way up, to fit me!!) And the hair, gotta have the hair, too, to complete the look.

Over six seasons, Carrie's 'do morphed from long, rock star curls; to sleek, chic chignons; to messy, chin-length bobs; to every imaginable style in between and never once looked less than fabulous. And perfect. Or fabulously perfect. Better yet, perfectly fabulous. I know, I've got to come up with different words, but you get the idea.

#4 THE GIRLS: More than anything else, I want to be Carrie Bradshaw because of "the girls," her gal-pal posse that is by her side for every triumph and tribulation. As Big puts it when he is asking the girls whether he should go to Paris to get Carrie, "You three know her better than anyone, you're the loves of her life, and a guy's just lucky to come in fourth."

There's Miranda Hobbes (Cynthia Nixon), the feisty, red-headed lawyer who favors logic over love, yet in the end gives in to love – and gives up Manhattan for Brooklyn! – when she marries sweet, sexy bartender Steve. Miranda is Carrie's go-to gal for advice on her biggest dilemmas and dramas, even though Carrie doesn't always like what she hears. Often cynical and acerbic but always well-meaning, Miranda is the only one of the girls that straight talks Carrie when she finds herself falling in big-time affair trouble with Big and later loses her "self" with Petrovsky. Just like Carrie, I sure can use a tough touchstone like Miranda from time to time.

There's also Charlotte York-MacDougal-York-Goldenblatt (Kristin Davis), the artsy, perpetually proper Park Avenue pal who believes true love exists and is forever finding ways to make it happen for herself and her friends. Just when Charlotte is on the verge of giving up – "I've been dating since I was 15. I'm exhausted! Where is he?" – she finds her Prince Charming in Dr. Trey MacDougal. Unfortunately, Charlotte's marriage to Trey doesn't last, just like Trey's erections. But, her Tiffany engagement ring rescues Carrie from having to live in her Manolos when her building goes condo, *and* Charlotte's divorce lawyer Harry Goldenblatt turns out to be the true love she kept believing in. Charlotte is exactly the cheerleader chum I need for life's rough spots. Maybe her money can't buy me happiness, but it can buy a lot of Cosmopolitans (the girls' pretty-in-pink signature drink) and that's a start.

I saved Samantha Jones (Kim Cattrall) for last. Because she's the best. With her free-wheeling sexuality ("I'm a trisexual. I'll try anything once.") and say-anything sauciness ("I'm dating a guy with the funkiest tasting spunk."), Samantha is the show's Next-Best-Thing-To-Sex dessert that you feel guilty about enjoying but eat every last bite of anyway. She loves sex. She loves her body. And she's not afraid to let both be known.

Samantha is beautiful, brazen, *and* eventually hooked up with boy-toy Smith Jerrod, a hung hottie that even hangs tight with her through breast cancer. Of all the girls, and I do love them all, I would choose to be Samantha if I can't get "Carrie-d away." (Being a public relations pro, Samantha can really pop a phrase, second only to CB. She used that play on words in Carrie and Big's rehearsal dinner toast. Couldn't resist borrowing it.)

***

So the other evening, my sweetie DMan is taking me out for a little wine tasting, then a wine-sipping visit with friends. An actual date night. Since most of my time is spent in grubby jeans and boring t-shirts for my job shelving books at the library, I decided to channel my inner Carrie and spiff up. I slipped on a hot pink bra, leaving an extra button undone on my silky black blouse for a pop of pink "accessory." I hauled out my gray high-heeled, faux-croc mock booties, that have been relegated to storage under the bed forever because they kill my feet, and paired them with dark boot-cut low-rider Levis. I mussed my hair and gave it a spritz of spray for that after-sex look Carrie pulls off so well. I even hauled out the makeup kit I mostly use for zit coverage and shadowed my eyes in shades of gray, lining my lids with the least dried-up eye pencil I could find. The final Carrie touch was a slick of pink lip gloss.

There. I had fixed myself up as close to Carrie as I would ever be. I looked in the mirror and . . . hideous looked back at me. After all that work, somehow I resembled a cheap hooker – one that is garishly exposed under the harsh glare of fluorescent lights at Walmart after a long, rode-hard night, no less – way more than the fabulous idol I was trying to emulate. The ancient eye liner was already flaking, leaving gray flecks on my cheeks. The shadow job I worked so hard on made my eyes look sunk in, as if I'd just been sprung from prison camp. The pink gloss gave my teeth a yellow(er) cast. The pink bra didn't even show unless I bent over completely since I have no cleavage to heave it out there. And then I nearly broke my neck in those heels trying to pirouette in front of the mirror to view this hideousness.

Before my obituary read "death by heels" or I frightened DMan off for good, I realized right then it was time to kiss Carrie Bradshaw good-bye. As much as I hated to, I had to finally admit it: I ain't never gonna be CB.

I'll never have her looks, no matter how much makeup I put on. I'll never pull off her perfectly put-together style, even if Patricia Field showed up at my house with a wardrobe truck full of Carrie's clothes in my size. My hair will always be too frizzy to be rock star curly and too curly to be sleek straight, so trying to have Carrie's 'do is a don't. I'll never lie next to Big and watch him blow smoke rings at the ceiling after smoking-hot sex, never have Seth dump me after sex, never get to cheat on Aidan with Big, never get the Post-it breakup from Berger, and never get to dance (horizontally or otherwise) and romance with Petrovsky. And the girls? The only time I'll get to have my own gal-pal posse like the girls is when I pop them in the DVD player. My

Carrie dream is over.

But wait. I *am* still a writer. That's my only shot at living the CB life. Now if I can just figure out a subject I know about that's as fabulous as her "Sex And The City" columns. Huh? What could it be? I do know a lot about Carrie Bradshaw and *Sex And The City*. What could be more fabulous than that?! And I do have six seasons worth of episodes, the *SATC: Kiss and Tell* official companion book, the trivia game, and *SATC – The Movie* for research material. This might work.

Don't pucker up yet, Carrie Bradshaw. The dream lives!

The

Craziest One

Of All

(Fall 2012)

Mirror, mirror

on the wall,

who's the craziest one of all?

The President of the United States!

November 6, 2012: Election Day. Seems like a good time to talk politics.

In case you've forgotten – amazing but true that we often forget about the also-rans before the winning candidate is even sworn in – this election has been a contentious battle between good and evil. I mean, Mitt Romney and Barack Obama. But it certainly played out as good versus evil in the media, social as well as news: Romney as the 31-flavors-of-conservative, quasi-

Christian (meaning Mormon, which *true* Christians say smacks of cult because Mormons have their own "bible"), corporate kiss-ass CEO white knight sent from Massachusetts to save the economy (and presumably the country) from the radical Islamic, cocaine-pushing, terrorist-lover, quasi-foreigner-turned-President Obama. And these were some of the nicer media descriptions of the candidates. I'm not kidding. I kept waiting for a photo of Romney walking on water to lay hands on a sick baby (because saving the economy makes for a lousy photo op) or leaked documents proving Obama bombed Pearl Harbor (he is from *Hawaii*, you know, it doesn't matter that he wasn't even born then).

Why either of these men would want to subject themselves to this kind of scandalous abuse is beyond me. Then, after months of torturous traveling, microscopic scrutiny, and televised debates worthy of Friday Night Smackdown status, the winner actually has to try to corral the folks that said such awful things about them in the first place and lead this monstrous mess of a nation. No way is being President worth it for a measly $400,000 a year, even with buff Secret Service agents forever at your beck and call (although that may be more of a perk when we finally have our first female

President!).

These guys must be crrr-azy to want the job. That goes for anyone running for any kind of public office. Politics has become an ugly business, where anything you have ever done or said or drank or smoked or voted for becomes fodder for the feeding frenzy of newspapers starved for paper-selling scandals, for "news" channels and websites dedicated to keeping the public informed (and inflamed) 24/7, and for your opponent to put in ads against you. Add to that all the stupid stuff the candidates do to sully *themselves*, such as having torrid affairs; not paying taxes and student loans owed to the very government they are trying to get a job with; participating in unscrupulous business deals; hiring illegal alien employees; and making ignorant comments like abortion should never be legal because "if it's a legitimate rape, the female body has ways to try to shut that whole thing down." (Many thanks to the former Missouri Republican Senate candidate Todd Akin who made this statement for making my home state seem even more red-neck and back-woods than people already think!) If all the smear campaign slogans and "breaking news" crawls are true, these people should not only NOT be candidates for office, most of them should be behind bars. I am a mostly squeaky clean gal – except for my predilection toward driving too fast and drinking too much red wine (but never at the same time!), plus my un-Christianlike living-in-sin lifestyle with my boyfriend DMan – but I wouldn't subject myself to the pains of politics to run for Dog Catcher, even if the job paid $400,000 and came with a free dog. And I love dogs.

So why do politicians do it?

That is *the* question that should be asked by the media and addressed in political ads, because the answer – if it's truthful, which is hard to guarantee when politicians are involved – would tell everything about the type of elected official they will become. Some run for power. You can see it in their eyes, that Grinch-like gleam from dreams of domination and manipulation of their minions. You can hear it in their speeches, subtle hints that "we the people" really means "me the people, in order to form pork barrel projects and do anything else I can get away with." That's scary, and sad. But even more sad are those politicians running because they actually believe they can change things and make a difference. As soon as they take office and have to work within our political system of back-scratching deals, PAC power, lobbyist-leaning legislation, and cover-your-ass-today-because-you'll-need-to-get-reelected-tomorrow mindsets, their demeanor changes even if nothing else does. They quickly morph from being a Saint Bernard, willing to charge into an avalanche to save a constituent, into being a tied-up mutt that lies down defeated in the dirt rather than run around in circles on a chain.

Sure, I'm exaggerating. Slightly. But there's enough truth there to make you cringe a little at the state our union is in, right?

So what can we do to fix it?

Mama says, "Give 'em six years in office. That's all. No reelection, no lifetime of sucking off the public teat in political office. If they can't do what they need to do in six years, then they didn't deserve to be in there in the first place."

Makes sense to me. Taking the whole issue of reelection out of the picture would allow our elected officials to actually focus on what they got elected to do and not spend half their term trying to get reelected. Elections would cost less because there would be less of them. Plus, there would be a steady stream of fresh ideas and new blood coming into office. Then maybe some things *would* change. Of course, it would take changing the laws to make the change in terms happen, which is not likely when the ones in charge are eager to keep their jobs.

My life buddy DMan wants to create a website called NoMud.com to counteract political ads. Candidates could only post what *they* believe in and are going to do in office. No smears, no slander against their opponent allowed. The site would also allow politicos to provide a defense against misleading ads. For example, let's say incumbent Senator SoandSo voted against a bill that would save all the cats in animal shelters from being euthanized. Sounds bad, huh? And Mr. Wannabea-Senator, his opponent, blankets the airwaves with commercials depicting cats marching into gas chambers under orders from Senator SoandSo. NoMud.com would give the Senator a neutral forum to set the record straight that his no-vote was because the bill also contained provisions that in order to save the cats, all the dogs in shelters had to be croaked. No one with any heart at all would vote for that bill. I hope.

NoMud.com would be the "Dragnet" of politics – just the facts, Ma'am. DMan's idea gets my vote. But I would take it even further. I mean, if we are going to shake things up, let's really make a fizz: NO MORE

POLITICAL ADS. Period. With newspapers, internet, and multiple channels of constant news, voters can find out all they need to know and more about the candidates and issues without billions (I'm guessing) being spent on paid advertisements. Most people ignore the ads anyway, just like I do.

Particularly in this election of 2012, one week before election day the entire northeast of the country was slammed by hurricane-turned-Super-Storm Sandy, which caused billions in damage. People were homeless, cold, and in the dark without basic necessities. Nearly 300 people died. Communities were devastated by floods, infrastructure was swept away, and sand dunes piled up where streets should be. And the rest of the country was flipping channels to avoid watching the political ads whose total cost could have paid for a hell of a lot of food, supplies, and clean up. That is a travesty.

Now if a couple of non-political nobodies like us can come up with such great ideas, just think about what the whole country could do. So I have one more suggestion: instead of asking on our income tax form if we want to donate $1 to the Presidential campaign that will be blown on costly but worthless ads, they should

Roni Blanche

ask if we want to contribute ideas on how to make the campaigns and the country better. I bet we crafty, concerned citizens could come up with some doozies worth much more than a buck. But keep the suggestions clean, please. Let's lead the way to putting civility back in politics.

November 7, 2012: The morning after. I am incredulous to wake up and hear that President Obama has been reelected. When I called it a night on all the election speculation, the networks were reporting people were still in line to vote in Florida, one of the key "battleground" states, and would be for several more hours. The Mountain and Pacific time zone states wouldn't close the polls for several hours as well. I figured this would turn into another 2000 Bush/Gore, count/recount, chad-hanging, days-long fight to the Florida-finish all over again, and I went to bed. So how can it be that the winner of the Presidential race could be "called" as early as 11:18pm Eastern Standard Time by the Associated Press when Ohio went for Obama? Is Ohio *the* crystal ball of the entire country? What about those poor patriots still standing in line at the polls – because supposedly EVERY VOTE COUNTS – when the

48

results were announced?! Something is very wrong with this picture.

In the spirit of full disclosure (not the usual spirit in politics, I know, but I'm hoping to start a trend here), I voted predominantly for democrats and yes, Obama was one of them. But despite there being a pretty clear victory with Obama's 332 electoral votes to Romney's 206, I'm not feeling any euphoric hallelujah moment from my candidate winning. This country is still a mess. People still need jobs. The economy is still iffy at best. Our soldiers are still dying in Afghanistan. The national debt is still growing by several billions every day. And if the world doesn't end on 12/21/12 when the Mayan calendar runs out, then our country is projected to fall off a "fiscal cliff" come January 2013 that sounds like the end of the world.

None of these things are going to change just because an election is over. The newly-elected politicians who slung so much mud at the opposing side are now going to have to work with that opposing side in order to honor their campaign promises and fix this country. So lest we citizens become the crrr-aziest ones of all in believing our leaders will accomplish anything at all without plenty of prodding (cattle or otherwise), it is up to us, whether we voted for them or not, to make our voices heard about how we want this country ran. Write letters. Send emails and tweets. Make phone calls. Share their voting record on Facebook (with all of the facts, please!) and post your like or dislike. Carve a huge message in the sand if you are still stuck without power in Super-Storm Sandyland. Our vote is only the beginning of our responsibility to our country because we've got crrr-azy people running our government.

Mirror, mirror
on the wall,
who's the crrr-aziest one of all?
We'll find out again in four more years.

Get Off

My Face

(Fall 2012)

Do you think about your looks? I do. I try not to, but still I do. The older I get, the less I like what I think about my looks. And what I see. My looks have gone to hell in a handbasket. Hell isn't pretty. The handbasket either.

I'll be the first to admit it: I've never been a pretty woman. Cute? Maybe. On a good day. In the right light. Interesting looking? Probably my best bet. I had the unlucky genetic draw to be dealt my dad's pronounced nose and chunky-knuckled, veiny man hands. They look fine on him. On me? Not so much. But I'm okay with that. Who needs the pressure of maintaining pretty anyway? It would require an endless siege against that relentless flesh-wrecker Mother Nature and her evil sidekick Dr. Gravity. One night of drunken splurging on all the infomercial gadgets and goos it would take to youth-anize my age spots, firm my flab, smooth my sags, and make my teeth Chiclet white would bankrupt me. So I'm just fine with being an average-Jane.

But there were times when I felt pretty good about my un-pretty self. Take good hair days, for instance. Even though I have a Medusa mop for hair – not curly enough for actual curls, not straight enough to be tamed into an actual style, more like a cascade of cowlicks – some days, when there was 0% humidity and I wasn't going anywhere anyway, I got lucky and it turned out just right. Those were feel-good days. I felt like I could fly on those days, no matter what shape the rest of me was in. Except that flying would have messed up my 'do.

My arms are another example. Years ago when I was doing massage therapy for a living and using my arms every day to muscle the knots and tension of out my clients, those babies dangling at my sides were a work of art. I was proud to don a sleeveless shirt and strut my toned triceps, defined deltoids, and beefed-up biceps. I would even be so bold as to say I was buff. Once. For a brief while.

Though I didn't have six-packs abs, I did have a waist and a flat(er) stomach. You could never bounce a quarter off my ass, but in my prime you might get a respectable recoil with a dime. And when I sported a tan to camouflage the cellulite, my legs looked damn fine. From a distance. In the right light. (When women get to a certain age, finding the right lighting becomes crucial. If you don't already know this, you will. Just wait. But you might want to start stockpiling candles now. Candles will become your best ally.)

Get Off My Face

But those feel-good days have gone bye-bye for good. Good hair now is when I get my hair-coloring day timed perfectly so the white roots don't show. My buff arms are covered in buff-colored crepey skin these days, complete with butt-crack armpit creases and Jello jiggles when they dangle at my sides. My current closet has mostly three-quarter sleeve or long sleeve shirts, with anything arm-revealing relegated to workout duty in the privacy of home. My waist is wider, my stomach squishy (and crepey, too, as if squishy wasn't bad enough), and the only thing you'd get off my ass nowadays is a soft sploink sound and a ripple effect no matter what coin you use. I still tan once a week to relax and treat myself to a hint of color, but unfortunately my "natural" glow turns the veins fronting my calves a God-awful green and highlights the hollows in my cottage-cheesy thighs. Ugh!

Nora Ephron, in the sadly true but oh so humorous essay "I Feel Bad About My Neck" from her book by the same name, said that for women everything goes soft and south when they hit age 55 no matter what they do. She was a damn fine writer (rest in peace, funny lady!) and I mean her no disrespect, but Nora, you got it way wrong. My downhill slide toward the

Savage "S"es (soft and south) started at 49. Now that I am 49-Part Two (I refuse to say I am 50. I had to write the actual number on a medical form the other day and it nearly gave me a stroke!), the slide has snowballed into an avalanche. Every morning I wake up sounding like a breakfast cereal advertisement, making a noisy snap (my ankles), crackle (my feet), and pop (my knees) with every step I take toward the bathroom instead of every bite. I don't even daydream about being young and spry anymore, I dream of wielding an oil can like Oz's Tin Man to lubricate away the creaks and pains. Sometimes I even say it out loud – "Oil can, oil can" – in a squeaky, lock-jawed voice when my joints are loudly protesting my every movement, but so far the magical motion potion hasn't materialized.

As much as it hurts to acknowledge how everything south of my neck has gone south with sags (and just plain old hurts some days), it's even worse to face my face. Whenever I inadvertently catch a glimpse of myself in the mirror – I never *advertently* look in the wretched thing – it scares the bejesus out of me. If my face is my window to the world, then I'm surprised children don't literally scream when they see me on the street from thinking the boogeyman is real and a chick and is walking around in broad daylight. Especially when I'm lost in thought (usually about my aching body or whether Medicare might cover facelifts if it is still around when I hit the jackpot age) or deep in one of my black funk doldrums (about feeling old, no doubt), my face becomes a swamp of sad sags. I'm not kidding. If I frown, which is unfortunately my natural facial state, I've got a crevasse in my chin deep enough to carry an echo. I do my best not to let my boyfriend DMan whisper sweet nothings near my chin for fear that the reverberating "I love you, I love you, I love you" might frighten him off for good.

   I used to wear eye shadow on those feel-good days or for date nights with DMan. No more. Somehow the browns and grays I was partial to started migrating into the creases below my lashes, and then people would ask me how I got the black eyes. Not what I wanted to hear when I took the extra time to glam up. And lipstick? I've given it up, too. No amount of liner will keep the color from seeping into the indentations spiking from my top lip that makes my lipstick job look like a three-year old's depiction of the stock market fluctuations. So I've reverted to my junior high makeup repertoire: mascara (waterproof, so it doesn't creep into the creases), moisturizer, and Bonne Bell Lip Smacker lip gloss (but in a more sophisticated Berry Peach now instead of teenybopper Dr. Pepper). I figured why try to do more if the results are only going to make me cry anyway. And I save money and time to boot.

I am also conserving cash since switching up my SJP NYC signature scent to MMR (Mentholated Muscle Rub) – no more perfume to buy. I do miss the sweet, sultry undertones of magnolia in the SJP NYC, but the zingy menthol both wakes me up and takes the edge off the aches. I just have to warn DMan not to get close to the lubed-up areas – neck, shoulders, low back, knees, feet – until the eye-smarting smell dissipates. That cuts down on our morning hugging and kissing routine, a bonus time saver.

Who knows, maybe by the time I reach Medicare age I will have saved enough to pay for my own nip-and-tuck (and vacuum the gobbler neck and plump the lips while you're at it, please!). If that doesn't work, maybe my mind will go south along with the rest of me, carry away all unhappy thoughts, and leave me with an instant wrinkle-lifting perma-grin. They say the mind is a terrible thing to waste, but it might be worth it if I get a free facelift out of the deal.

I joke about aging because I don't need anything else making me frown, but really I am angry. It feels like I am being punished for attempting to age naturally as a woman without turning myself into a waxified, monster-like caricature of my youthful self in this era when looking young is prized above all else and when some people that are even older than me (Cher, by 16 years) look younger and better now than I *ever* did (Cher). It's just not fair (Cher!).

I'm reminded of a gripping scene from the funny yet poignant movie classic *Guess Who's Coming To Dinner*. Sidney Poitier, playing Dr. John Wade Prentice, is the "who" that's coming to dinner at the home of the much younger white woman he wants to marry. Keep in mind that the film was made in 1967, when black + white = illegal in many states, so her otherwise liberal white parents were shocked and his conservative black parents were downright appalled at the coupling. The scene that keeps playing in my mind is when the doctor's father is berating him for making the biggest mistake of his life by breaking society's rules in wanting to marry outside his color. Mr. Poitier's character angrily responds:

"You don't own me! You can't tell me when or where I'm out of line, or try to get me to live my life according to your rules. You don't even know what I am, Dad, you don't know who I am. You don't know how I feel, what I think. And if I tried to explain it the rest of your life you will never understand. You are thirty years older than I am. You and your whole lousy generation believes the way it was for you is the way it's got to be. And not until your whole generation has lain down and died will the dead weight of you be off our backs! You understand, you've got to get off my back!"

What a powerful punch of dialogue! I know the movie is dated, but if you haven't seen it, it's a must watch for anyone that loves Katharine Hepburn, Spencer Tracy, or Poitier! Anyway, when I'm hearing that scene in my head, it becomes *me* blasting out those words at society and the media for setting the impossible standard that while the population is growing increasingly older, we women are expected to look young forever or else become an embarrassing eyesore blighting the world of the beautiful rule-following people. And, I am lambasting Mother Nature and Dr. Gravity to get their dead weight off my back. Only I realize that my back is one of the few parts of me that has held up pretty well – at least what I can see of it in the damn mirror without my glasses – so instead, you two GET OFF MY FACE! Just lay down and die and leave me alone to age and ache in peace. Please?!

Until my speech starts working or my facelift ship comes in, I'll carry on with my mentho-masca-rizer routine, with a side of lip gloss and the occasional apricot scrub (I think of it like taking a chance on a lottery scratch-off ticket and maybe one day I'll get lucky and all that scrubbing will reveal a whole new face). Might be a good idea to watch the movie again and then practice my spiel in the mirror to give it an extra punch. Oh no, the mirror, the dreaded mirror. I know, I'll practice in the mirror by candlelight. Everything looks better in the soft flicker of candles. Even *my* face.

Roni Blanche

(The "You've got to get off my back" scene from
the movie *Guess Who's Coming To Dinner*)

No thanks,

I'll pass

(Winter 2014)

No thanks, I'll pass. On passing out, that is. Have you heard about these folks that pass out *on purpose*? Auto-asphyxiation it's called, or erotic asphyxiation if done during sex. From what I've read, the pass-out junkies put something over their faces or clamp off their windpipes until the sudden loss of oxygen creates an endorphin-release high and sense of giddiness before the unconsciousness sets in. In the erotic version, the black-out process reportedly increases sexual pleasure and amps up the orgasm. I have passed out three times in my life – not during sex, though, I try to stay awake for that – and all I ever got was perspiration, puke, and pee. And embarrassment, major embarrassment. Maybe I wasn't doing it right. You be the judge.

Pass Out #1

A hot September, definitely Indian summer, found me living back home in Missouri with my parents after leaving my first husband. In need of a job and a place to live in a hurry – I love Mama and Daddy, I do, but not to live with – I decided a spiffy new hairdo would boost my confidence and be a first step into my new solo life. I tracked down an old friend from high school who had

65

become a super stylist, and she gave me the glam
treatment: haircut, mousse job, blow dry, curling
ironing, and a final shellacking with hairspray that could
withstand a wind tunnel. I looked fabulous!

Before meeting Mama at her work at Montgomery
Ward and then having lunch together at Orange Julius, I
took my new "do" out to run errands, check out
apartments, and give blood. That last item might seem
like an odd thing to do, but since I had moved away
from Missouri I hadn't donated blood once and felt
guilty. Word of caution: Be careful what you feel guilty
about because it may rear up and bite you in the ass.

Even though I was running around like a chicken
with its head cut off, I got everything done and made it
to the store even before time for Mama's lunch break.
She parked me in an empty back office to wait for her.
No problem, I can amuse myself and rest a bit. I
plopped on a 1950s metal desk, dangled my legs, and
hummed a Skynyrd tune so as not to hear my stomach
growling. I had declined the offer of a post-donation
snack in order to save my calories for lunch. The Red
Cross had some fine snacks, too: Little Debbie Nutty
Bars and Oatmeal Creme Pies, Goldfish crackers, and
orange drink that tasted just like Tang. What a dummy I

was to skip all that.

I grabbed a Ward's sales circular and began thumbing through to get my mind off food. Not a good distraction, though, too much reminder of the clearance-rack clothes Mama always bought that made me feel even more uncool than I already was in high school. I decided to head on down to Orange Julius and wait for her there.

I jumped off the desk to go tell Mama my plan and . . . WHOA NELLIE! The room started to spin and took me with it. My gut bottomed out, leaving me feeling hollow as a gourd inside. Intense heat radiated from my empty belly through my entire body. Sweat beads popped out like a dam had burst, especially on my freshly-coiffed scalp. The store sounds turned muffled as if I had dived underwater. The last thing I heard was a dull thud as my forehead slammed into a steel Army-surplus filing cabinet, which was just my height. Wasn't that nice for it to "catch" me like that and save me from falling face down onto the concrete floor?

Faces I didn't know were staring down at me when my eyes opened. A lady was fanning me with a summer catalog, another wiped my face with a damp paper towel. I wasn't sure where I was, but I was sure that every piece of my clothing was stuck to whatever I was lying on as if I had just taken a shower fully dressed. The mouths on the faces above me were moving, but my ears still weren't working right. I tried to unstick myself and get up, but black splotches floated before my eyes and even more sweat poured out of me, a river of it running down my scalp and pooling under my neck. I stayed put.

After more fanning and dabbing and a couple sips of ice water brought to my lips by a grandmotherly gal, my ears cleared and the splotches stopped floating.

"Are you alright?" I heard from the water lady. "My goodness, we heard a racket of banging and crashing in the receiving office and found you keeled over flat on the floor. You must've hit your head hard, look at that welt coming up on your forehead. What in the world were you doing in there? And who in the world are you?"

I croaked out Mama's name, the only words I could muster, and somebody went to fetch her from major appliances. Without needing a mirror, seeing Mama's face told me "whatever happened was bad and I looked even worse."

Her face wasn't kidding. When I was finally

steady enough to extricate myself from the sweaty vinyl sofa in the ladies lounge, bathroom mirrors were everywhere. My fancy hairdo was plastered to my head in the back and on one side, shellacked now with hairspray *and* sweat, while the other side was still styled and poofy. I looked like both the "before" and "after" pictures in a makeover magazine at the same time. The filing cabinet impression on my forehead was plumping like a hot dog under the skin, quickly morphing from blood red to bruised plum. My eye makeup, which I took extra time with that morning to accent the new hairstyle, had run halfway down my face in a waterfall of sweat. And my clothes? They hung on me as if I'd put them on soaking wet straight out of the washing machine.

Turns out you shouldn't run around all morning on a hot day and an empty stomach, give blood, and then get up too fast. Not unless you want to pass out cold, ruin your 'do, and resemble a drowned rat. Not unless you like being carried to the ladies lounge by two burly warehouse dudes you don't even know, driven home by your daddy because you can't see straight, then fill your belly and crash for five hours before you feel like yourself again. Take my word for it.

Pass Out #2

Trying to pack too many to-dos into too little time makes me crazy, but it's just my way of doing things. This day was no exception.

I was scheduled to do a one-to-five shift at my receptionist gig at a day spa, then I would see two massage therapy clients of my own there afterward. That would shoot the afternoon and evening, but I had decided that I could still cram more into my morning. After doing the household chores I deemed "necessary" – most likely laundry or grocery buying, I don't remember – I got in an hour of aerobics with a workout DVD and worked up a hellacious sweat. And appetite.

Besides all that it was time to give blood again, and today was the day. The Community Blood Center's promo to kick off the summer donation drive was on its last day, and I wanted the giveaway t-shirt. Bad. The caption read, "'Iguana' give blood. I did, I did give blood!," surrounded by dancing iguanas in fiesta-colored sombreros and serapes. Just the kind of funky casual wear that I love. So, after a quick shower, I hauled ass to the CBC. My heart must have been pumping like an oil derrick at warp speed, because I was done donating in record time. Having learned my lesson from the Monkey Ward's incident, I even sipped some faux Tang and nibbled a few Goldfish crackers before leaving.

Perfect. I still had time to grab a tuna sandwich and Cheddar Sun Chips at Subway on the way to work. Perfect day as well, with a cloudless blue sky and low humidity, to have my lunch picnic-style on the stoop outside the spa's back door and soak up some sun.

The tuna and chips were delish, at least from what I tasted while scarfing them down and watching my watch. Still had time for a quick cigarette before work. Nothing like a smoke to settle my stomach after a meal, which was a bit jumpy from all the running around.

If you're not a smoker, you wouldn't have experienced that having a cigarette after a couple of drinks (of the alcoholic variety) seems to intensify the buzz. It's true, light up and all of a sudden you feel more drunkety drunk. So I'm not sure if it was the effect of having a smoke, smoking too fast, eating too fast, or all of the above plus pumping out my blood sprint-style while donating, but when I stood up to go into work I got a major head-rush and it was WHOA NELLIE time again. Here came the popping sweat, racing heart, hollow gut, and underwater ears. This time I knew exactly what was happening. It didn't help. I plopped down on my butt HARD on the stoop, and that's all I remember.

Sometime later, I do remember thinking I was dead. I heard soft, heavenly music when my ears woke up. Everything was dark except for a faint glow around me. I was lying on something cushy, cocooned by a blanket. *This is my funeral, I am in a coffin* popped into my head, which pissed me off because I had expressly asked to be cremated. Then someone touched me on the shoulder. I sat up with a jolt and the room spins. No, I wasn't dead but wished I was. Especially after Sheila, the spa owner who had touched my shoulder to see if I was awake, filled in the disgusting details of my black out.

According to her, when I plopped down I must have keeled over sideways, my face coming to rest ever so UN-gently on the cement. Despite the crimson bullseye on my cheek, this was really quite fortunate as I then upchucked my picnic all over the stoop. Had I passed out on my back, I might have drowned in my own vomit, or if I had slumped forward, I certainly would have soiled my outfit. So it could have been worse.

No thanks, I'll pass

When I wasn't at my desk by one o'clock, Sheila came looking for me in my usual smoking spot and found me when the back door hit my inert body. She and another massage therapist helped me to a therapy room – she claimed I was able to walk, but that was news to me – put me on the massage table, lit some candles, covered me up because I was drenched in sweat, and let me sleep it off.

I am proud to say that I did manage to finish the last two hours of my shift after a long snooze, even with hair that looked like a cow had lick-styled it and my body smelling of eau de sweat. Luckily, there is dim lighting for ambiance in the reception area so maybe none of the clients noticed my "hair-don't," and I kept a candle burning on my desk to squelch my stench. I am embarrassed to say that I didn't have enough mojo to massage my clients and I bailed out on them. And I'm ashamed to say I did not thank the person who policed up my puke. I didn't even ask who did it; I just couldn't. But the next time I had a stoop smoke the evidence was gone, leaving only a whiff of tainted tuna in the sweltering summer air to remind me of the picnic-upchuck pass-out.

Pass Out #3

My blood-giving days are over. No, I wasn't banned for being an idiot and passing out twice, although I probably should have been since my post-donation dramas, while amusing (now), don't bode well for enticing new donors. No, I would still love to be able to offer my blood, but I am considered a "permanent deferral" due to a diagnosis I was given when a doctor was trying to rule out my having tuberculosis. Damn doctors don't know how to mind their own business. I don't have TB, never did have. And I don't consider myself to have the diagnosed ailment either. But still I was honest in my disclosure with the blood donation place, therefore the ban stands. So now I donate plasma. And get paid for it. I guess honesty does pay off in the long run.

I've got this plasma-donation routine down too. My appointments are scheduled for my days off or after work, that way I'm not overtaxing my body. I take a quickie nap after donating, leaving me feeling refreshed and not drained the rest of the day. Plus, I amp up my hydration and protein intake on plasma days, two key components of a successful donation. Over a decade had passed since my last pass-out, and I'd never had an issue with donating plasma until . . . I monkeyed with the routine.

Why I did things differently, I don't recall. Probably a case of post-plasma pass-out amnesia impeding my memory. But this day, instead of sleeping in since it was my day off, I got up early and rushed around working out and writing. Instead of having my protein smoothie just before leaving to donate, I drank it right after I woke up and ate nothing else the entire morning. Despite feeling a might hungry and tired, my donation went fine. I was feeling so fine that I had a quickie smoke on the drive home even though they recommend waiting for an hour after the donation. No problem, I thought, I have this down pat.

I thought wrong. Standing up to get out of my car when I got home, the woozies set in. DMan came into the kitchen to greet me, and his sturdy hug settled me down. I just need to eat something, I told myself, and I'll be all better. Wrong again. I slapped chunky peanut butter on a slice of bread, folded it over, and nibbled it over the sink. My knees buckled after three bites, and I grabbed the sink. The sound of DMan's noon news from the TV started fading in my ears. After a fast flash of heat, sweat started to pour despite my being chilled from the donation-ending flush of saline and frigid temperature outside. I *WAS* right about one thing: I was going down.

But I didn't hit the ground. Thankfully. Otherwise DMan would have heard the thud, come running, and witnessed the unfolding spectacle. Instead, my body jackknifed into the sink, my feet barely touching the floor, and my forehead came to rest on the plastic mat covering the garbage disposal. Somehow my mind was working enough to say, "Chew, chew. Don't swallow or you'll choke." I kept chewing in SLOOOOW motion, face down in the sink, the wad of doughy peanut butter swelling more in my mouth with every chew. Then I felt another flash of warmth, this time down my thighs. My bladder had blacked out as well, and I was powerless to stop the trickle of pee saturating my jeans. When things go wrong for me, they go WAY wrong. But at least my bowels didn't buckle like my knees and bladder.

I have no idea how long I was "inSinkerated." My ears waking up are always my sign that I am coming to, and eventually I could hear DMan laughing at *The Andy Griffith Show* that comes on after the news. *Thank God, he doesn't know I keeled over into the sink.* I slowly un-jackknifed myself, the half-eaten sandwich still in my fist, my back stiff from being bent over. The chaw of peanut butter in my cheek had swelled to the size of a lime, but I hadn't swallowed! I tried to spit it out, then flick it out with my tongue. Nothing happened. It was stuck. I finally had to rake two fingers along the inside of my cheek to extricate the gluey glob. My jeans had trapped the tinkle so I wasn't standing in a puddle, but by now the wetness was cold. Shivery cold.

As quietly as I could with soaked pant legs rubbing together, I slipped through the sitting room and into the bathroom. DMan didn't notice, still engrossed in Mayberry antics in the living room. Have Mercy, I was a fright: hair plastered back from my face with sweat, showcasing a red checker-boarded forehead the spitting image of the sink mat; mascara smeared into raccoon eyes; sweat rings surrounding my armpits; and a dark rainbow of urine on my jeans from crotch to calf. After cleaning myself up and hosing down my pants in the shower, I took a long nap, more like a mini-coma, and vowed never to monkey with my plasma routine again. Never.

So now you understand why I say, "No thanks, I'll pass on passing out." I don't know about those "asphyxionados," but I never had a bit of fun in passing out. No endorphin high. No giddiness. And I sure as hell never got an orgasm out of the deal. I must have been doing it wrong. WAY wrong.

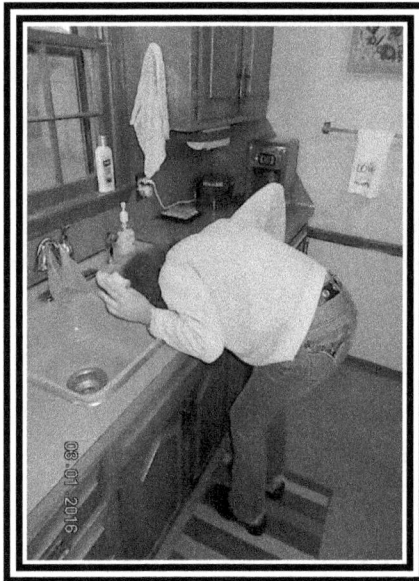

(A reenactment of my inSinkeration, complete with peanut butter sandwich but without the urine rainbow. When I asked DMan to take the photo, he said, "I didn't know you passed out in the sink." Guess I made a clean – except for the pee – getaway that day.)

Tit

for

Tat

(Late Summer 2013)

Tit for Tat

(One of my coffee sunrise walks from when
I lived at the beach. Now that's the way
to start my day out right!)

When you think about it, life is a tangle of trade-offs, a karmic tit for tat that is paid with every choice we make. While I try *not* to think about my trade-offs too much – dwelling on them only makes them seem worse – lately I can't escape it. Maybe it's because the older I get the clearer I see that my life has been shaped by the trade-offs I've made and, as my gal pal Carrie Bradshaw would say, I couldn't help but wonder if I made good trades.

Roni Blanche

Two years ago I left my full-time, workaday "normal" life and skedaddled to the beach to be a writer. These dreams, of being a beach babe and writing, had been festering under the surface for years until they finally spewed over and I made them my reality. I loved that life: walking the beach every day and having things to write about hit me like sea gull plop; being nurtured by Mother Ocean when I felt lonely; my days bookmarked by coffee sunrises and wine sunsets, and flowing in between with the rhythm of the tide; the wild swings of weather and my writer mojo. And I hated it too. The disappointment of winter finding me even at the beach, and the sting of receiving rejections – or worse yet, no response at all – to all my writer efforts, both robbed my spirit of the joy of living my dreams. Even though I lived a modest beach existence, the teeny cash cushion I had from my recent divorce quickly dwindled into the danger zone, my lottery tickets were all losers, and my writing was costing money in contest entry fees and postage for submissions and queries to publishers while never earning a dime. Eventually, I had shot my financial wad. Plus, I missed my sweetie DMan. It became time to give up the beach babe dream and go home.

Tit for Tat

So here I am once again living in land-locked Missouri. Sure, there are lakes close enough that I can be near the water if I feel the need, can find some peace in the splish splash of ripples hitting the shore from time to time. But visiting a lake can never match the mighty roll of Mother Ocean's waves, the serenity of warm sand on bare feet, the cooling of a beach breeze while the sun melts like butter on my skin.

Good trade or not? Was I right to go and experience my dream life even if only for a short time, store up memories, and short-circuit the regret of never having tried? Or would I be better off to have never lived the beach life, never realized how perfectly it fit me and that I felt *home* finally, and never be missing it all the more now because it *WAS* my existence, my reality?

I let go of the beach life so I wouldn't be homeless and starving, but I couldn't give up being a writer. There is a scene I love in the movie *Thelma and Louise* when the ladies are contemplating giving up running from the law and Thelma says, "It's like something's crossed over in me and I can't go back, you know? I just couldn't live." Yes, I do know. I couldn't fathom going back to the spirit-sucking, eight-to-five grind and not having any time or mental mojo left to write. So I took a part-time job at the library, at first shelving books and then later checking them in and out. The work doesn't pay much and offers no benefits. My body feels rode hard and put up wet by the time my shift ends. Despite what folks may think, library work ain't for wussies: it's a full-body workout of bending, squatting, lifting, pushing heavy carts, and walking A LOT. But when I clock out, I'm done. No work or worries to take home that would interfere with my creativity.

Sounds pretty great, huh? It is. And it isn't. Fear gets a grip on me every time I have an unexplainable pain, every time my allergies flare up and I'm headed for asthmatic bronchitis again no matter what I do. I have no insurance, no extra cash to pay for a doctor visit. So I worry, concoct my own over-the-counter cocktail of remedies, and hope that someone in my family has had bronchitis, too, so I can bum an inhaler and breathe again. Even though I know it's coming, my gut clenches when my car insurance bill arrives in the mail, my oil needs changing, or my brakes need work. Then some other bill (or buying food or restocking my anti-allergy arsenal) will have to wait in order to cover the extra expenses. No car = no getting to work = no money, period.

Tit for Tat

My life buddy DMan would help me out financially in a heartbeat if I was in dire straits, a blessing many in my situation don't have. But I already feel like Freida Freeloader, relying on him to cover the majority of our rent and household expenses. For an independent woman like myself, that's a choking chunk of pride to swallow without asking for even more help. The faint light at the bottom of the poor-me pit is the Mega Millions lottery ticket I buy twice a week. I kiss it, tuck it under the hot pink Myrtle Beach magnet on the fridge, and recite my mantra: *Come on, Baby, be a winner. Roni needs to go to the dentist. Roni needs a mammogram. Roni needs to go to the beach.*

Good trade or not? Is the freedom of part-time, not-all-consuming work, which allows me the time and energy to write, worth the constant fear of what-ifs that I can't afford or control?

Speaking of work trade-offs, I have a friend who has worked in the insurance industry for 30-plus years. The job is demanding, but he gets paid well, gets to travel and enjoy perks like a company car. He is very good at his work and seems to like it fine most days. Yet my friend cannot wait to retire and counts down the weeks even though he has several working years ahead.

But he's not pining for the big pension checks or more free time or moving to Florida though. No, none of the usual "when I retire" dreams for my friend. *He can't wait to smoke pot again.* Yes, you read that right. His retirement nirvana is to be free of drug tests and fire up a big old joint any time he wants.

Now I have never been a big fan of pot (if you've read the chapter "Who The Hell Am I?" already, you'll understand why), but it seems sad to me to devote all your working life to a job which requires that you deny yourself something you enjoy so much that you can't wait to retire to be able to enjoy it again. That is one whopper of a sentence, I know, but it nutshells one whopper of a tit for tat!

Instead of only feeling sad for him, though, I try to imagine the huge grin on his face as he fires up his first post-retirement, Cheech-and-Chong-worthy doobie and inhales deeply. What I can't imagine is how he will score some pot after being out of the dope scene for over 30 years. Will I spot him hanging around outside a high school, looking like someone's grandpa, while he's trying to spot the "heads" with a dime bag to sell? (Do they even call it a dime bag anymore? It's probably up to 50 bucks by now, considering inflation.) Will he be googling old partying pals to see if they are still alive and, if so, do they still have pot or connections? Or maybe I should look more closely at the "herb" garden he's been cultivating all these years? There may be way more than parsley, sage, rosemary and thyme in there. No matter how he gets his dream doobie, I hope the trade was worth it and the high is the best of his life.

If I thought giving up dreams made for tough trade-offs, that is nothing compared to the minefield of tit for tat in intimate relationships. Could this be the reason breakups and divorces get so explosive? You make what you think are good trades for the sake of love, then when the relationship goes bad, you are resentful as hell and feel like a sucker. You want back what you traded, but there are no takesies-backsies in breakup-land.

I am reminded of a scene from *Sex And The City – The Movie* when the ladies are lamenting about their men troubles after Carrie got jilted by Big at the alter. Samantha Jones, the original I-only-want-men-for-sex Ms. Independent, who had now been in a five-year relationship with hubba hubba Smith Jerrod, opens up to the gals and says:

"As long as we're going down this road, I can't believe my life revolves around a man. On what planet did I allow that to happen?"

Sweet Charlotte, who believes in love at any cost, says, "But you love him."

Samantha continues, "Does that mean saying his name 50 times more a day than I say my own? Does it mean worrying about him and his needs before me and mine? Is it all about the other person? Is that love?"

Besides being the girlfriend, Samantha is also superstar actor Smith Jerrod's PR person in Hollywood, so that brings a whole new tangle to their relationship tango. But she makes valid points. It's those little everyday "tits" that can stick in your craw and go sour. Like always saying "he" or "we" instead of "me." Like making sure he has 2% milk for his coffee because he won't drink your soy milk. Like yawning every other breath through *The Tonight Show with Jay Leno* – which you find so NOT funny – even though you are dog tired because *he* likes to stay up late and then fall asleep together, while you much prefer falling asleep when you are sleepy, even if that means alone. Like making yourself watch golf or baseball or Nascar on TV yet again – and being bored out of your gourd yet again – in order to spend time with your man while a fabulous book you are dying to read lies unopened on the coffee table right in front of you. And yes, as you've probably already guessed, the above was all about me. I am the "you" I was talking about.

On the flip side, my sweetie DMan has silently suffered through several viewings of *Sex And The City – The Movie* and patiently listened as I pointed out my favorite scenes (what scene isn't my favorite?!) and quoted the dialogue out loud when I know he would rather be watching golf, baseball, or Nascar. Even The Weather Channel. Anything but *SATC*. Again.

And those trade-offs are nothing compared to what he puts up with when I fall into one of my black funk depressions! I've often thought the man must be a saint. Or sometimes I wonder if there is some deep, dark, karmic debt he's paying off by being in a relationship with me. That makes me feel a bit better about being such a pain in the patootie to live with.

What about the issue of living together? What about giving up soloness for togetherness? For some folks, *that* would be a dream come true, having someone to spend their lives with. For me, it's one more tit for tat. When I lived at the beach and he lived here in Missouri, DMan and I often imagined what kind of extraordinary, ordinary moments we might share if we lived together: a spontaneous dance while cleaning house and listening to 70s tunes; seeing a cardinal land on a snowy branch outside the kitchen window as we unload the dishwasher on a dreary day; a giggle-fest and water fight erupting while we wash our cars side by side in the driveway. So we moved in together when I came back home. And now? Sure, we enjoy our shared moments, lots of them. But besides work, the news, the weather, our "What kind of wine shall we drink tonight?" convos, and reliving those shared moments, we don't have much to talk about. I miss that "I can't wait to see him to tell him something that happened" feeling from when we were just dating. I miss craving him when I hadn't seen him in a few days. I miss getting that jolt of tingles when he would pull in my driveway because I knew in just a minute he'd have his big, hot hands all over me. I miss the urgency, the intensity that came from missing him.

If piddly things like these stick in your craw and

go sour, the big things can eat at your craw like battery acid until eventually they devour you completely. Big things like moving somewhere you don't want to live, making a home in a place that doesn't feel anything like home so your significant other can take a promotion. Important things like having kids because that's what couples are *supposed* to do, then finding out that your whole life together revolves around the kids' lives and, besides orthodontist appointments and soccer games, you have absolutely nothing to say to each other. Monumental things like leaving your career to be a mom, then wondering when your oldest kid graduates high school whether you would have made vice-president if you had kept working. Or, finally getting the huge partner office with a spectacular view, yet your gut aches when you have nothing to hang on the walls but the diplomas and certificates that got you there because you didn't have time to have a career AND a family. Those are some big tits that some people have to live with, no matter how good the tats seem.

But the ultimate in trade-offs comes with death. Or life, and the choices between the two. Because Mama is what she calls a "prayer warrior," I am constantly bombarded with details about the folks she is praying for and their serious health problems, surgeries, treatment regimens, and prognoses. The ones that hit me the hardest are the ones with cancer. What kind of choices are they given?

Should they choose to fight and, in doing so, mangle their body with surgery, poison their cells with chemo, and burn their flesh with radiation? Must they accept indiginities and suffering as part of the battle in the hope they can beat the cancer and win? For how long? At what cost?

Or should they surrender to the havoc of cells gone crazy, to an unknown path that may meander through pit stops of organ failure, bloating, wasting, suffocating, and dementia? Should they just live with indiginities and suffering as a condition of armistice with the Big-C in the hope that it will miraculously retreat or mercifully kill them quick? How long will they wait to know their fate? At what cost?

In my mind, there is no question of choice. I have pondered long and hard over the years about what I would do if I got a cancer diagnosis – either this is a natural side-effect of hearing about so many people with cancer or I am just one morbid chick with too much time to think – and, unless the invader is something small and easily removed, I *won't* fight it. Screw surgery. Screw treatments. Whatever time and health I have left *will* be spent laughing and celebrating with my special peeps. I *will* play disco music too loud and dance until I collapse satisfied. I *will* eat, drink, and smoke anything I want to my heart's content. And I *will* spend every last buck I've got to scratch off every last want-to-do from my bucket list. Since life for death is THE final trade-off, I'm going to be sure I make every trade I have left a good one, and hopefully make peace with the not-so-good trades I've already made along the way.

My terminal tit for tat. Hope I get it right. Or better yet, hope I get hit by a big-ass bus and . . . SPLAT! Just like that, the end of me and tits for tats.

Why Didn't

My Mother

Have Me

Tested?

(Spring 2015)

(Jim Parsons, playing Dr. Sheldon Cooper,
on *The Big Bang Theory*.)

A freak. Weird. Abbie-normal, as Mama says. That's how I've felt about myself all my life, that there was something *seriously* not right about me. Why didn't I think and act like normal folks? Was I just uber quirky or truly crazy?

Speaking of crazy, my *Big Bang Theory* buddy Dr. Sheldon Cooper gets asked if he is crazy all the time because of his Asperger-esque quirks. He is lucky, though, and doesn't have to wonder. After several

childhood incidents, like Sheldon building a death ray –
which didn't scare the neighbor kids, as intended, but
"pissed their dog off to no end" – and trying to buy
yellow-cake uranium off the internet to build his own
nuclear reactor, his mother, Mary Cooper, a sweet but
righteously religious Texan with a mild Dr. Pepper
addiction, had Sheldon checked out by professionals.
Now, whenever he gets asked, he can confidently reply,
"I'm not crazy. My mother had me tested."

While I never had any interest in death rays or
reactors, there were certainly foreshadowings of my
freakdom to come. *Mama, did you not notice that by the
second day after school was out for the summer I was
already bored and clamoring for something to do? Were
you not at all concerned that I didn't play dress-up or
play with dolls like other girls, didn't play with anything
really, just kept my nose in a book and had
conversations with MYSELF when I wasn't reading? Did
it not seem unusual, if not downright bizarre, that
despite being a constant babysitter to my sisters and
the neighborhood kids, I HATED KIDS? All kids? Even
myself because I was a kid?*

*Honestly Mama, was there no alarm bell going off
or red flag flying when, no matter where I was or what I*

was doing, I was always wishing I were somewhere else? Doing something, anything else?

With all these clues that I was crazy, I had to wonder: Why didn't my mother have me tested?

To be fair, money was always scarce in my family. Feeding four children on an Army sergeant's salary wasn't easy, especially when buying a new car every year was a priority. My dad traded cars like boys trade baseball cards, as a hobby. Of course he always had the safety and comfort of the family in mind, like the time he traded our purple Plymouth station wagon – that thing was as big as a yacht, with room in the middle for my baby sister's playpen and a backward-facing rear seat big enough to hold me, my other two sisters, plus some neighbor kids – for a hot-orange, two-door GTO Judge sporting the Firebird emblem on the hood. It had a stick shift that pounded my knees because I had to ride between my parents in the front seat to fit all of us kids in, plus black leather seats that melted our naked legs in the summer but NO AIR CONDITIONER. The best part was the decorative license plate that read "Chicken Shift." (It sounded like cussing when I said it fast and I was all about sneaking in cuss words to my vocab!) We were cramped and hot in that GTO, but we looked cool riding around town!

You are probably thinking my crazy apple didn't fall far from Daddy's wacko tree, right? Well, Amen to that, but back to the money issue. No, we didn't have a cache of cash to blow but we did live on an Army post from my first grade through seventh grade years. There was a humongous hospital right down the road from our quarters, offering all the free medical care we could ever want. So I'm begging to know: *Mama, why didn't you have me tested?*

My entire life could have been different if only I had known, like Sheldon, that I wasn't crazy. Or if I WAS bonkers, if I had known what pill I could pop or treatment I could take to get better. Even if the testing showed I was abso-freakin'-lutely insane, I wouldn't have minded being locked up. Three hots and a cot with a side order of mind-blowing meds sounds better than spending all my life trying to seem normal when I felt like a freakazoid.

By now you must be wondering what form of freakazoidal tendencies I am talking about. To save your time and my embarrassment, I won't even drone on (much) about all my physical flaws, such as my Dumbo ears. Well, really they aren't so much large as they are protruding. Like wings. Seriously, on a windy day the inside of my head roars like a wind tunnel, and I am shocked I don't actually take flight. Lucky for me I have thick, poofy hair that generally hides the offensive (to me anyway) flappers. Now if I could only quit whacking on my bangs I might be able to cover up my newest peculiarity: sweaty brows. Even when I am NOT in the midst of a super-hottie moment (aka hot flash), huge beads of perspiration pop up on my eyebrows and lids, causing me to constantly dab, dab, dab at my eyes with a tissue so folks don't fear I'm going to squirt them with my brows like a circus clown does with a fake flower.

Those external flaws are bad enough, but it gets worse. Unfortunately, the nature of my more concerning abbie-normalities cannot be concealed by a coiffure, so I might as well spill them: I AM a fickle flake and I AM NOT truly a chick. See, all those freakish childhood behaviors were a foreshadowing of the full-blown freak I was to become.

First to the fickle flake facets of me. As much as I hate it – and hate to admit it! – I am flaky as a bisquit when it comes to sticking with things. Anything. Everything. Take jobs, for instance. In my 36 years of working, I have had 24 jobs. 24! My life buddy DMan just hit his 24th year with the same employer, and I am on my 24th different job. People I went to high school with are starting to retire after spending 30-some years doing the same work. Even if I stuck with one job starting today, I'd be nearly 90 before I could ever retire. While they've been work horses, I've been a work whore.

It's not that I am a bad employee. I have never been fired or even laid off, and I have totally kicked ass in any job I've ever had. Call my past employers, they'll tell you: Roni kicked ass.

So what went wrong? I wish I knew. Every job started out perfect, just the right thing for me. Then something changed: the hours, the workload, the stress level, the people. Something. Then the job wasn't so perfect anymore and disallusionment set in.

At one point in my life I thought social work was my true calling, a way to help people, my means of doing something good in the world. My first job in that field was working with families who had kids in foster care. Yes me, working with kids. Crazy, huh, since I don't even like kids? Even crazier than that was I managed to tolerate the kids, and the kids *liked* me. Or maybe they just faked it pretty good. Either way, I was tooling along, thinking "I've got this social work thing whooped. This may be IT for me."

Then something changed. My caseload kept getting larger and larger, while my clients kept getting meaner and scarier. Like the big mama from California – and I do mean BIG, she was built like a wrecking ball atop spindly legs – who had F-U-C-K delicately prison-tattooed across both knuckles and who threatened to kill me if anything happened to her precious little angels while in foster care. Never mind that her two angelic daughters, both under the age of five, were only in state custody because she had left them alone in a homeless shelter for three days while she road-tripped out of state to "take care of some business."

Then there was a dad who wrote these lengthy treatises to me from prison – addressing all his letters "Dear Larry" despite being repeatedly reminded that my name was Roni – about how he was an alpha male and would "take me out" if I took his son away by terminating his parental rights. Somehow Mr. Alpha Male ignored the fact that his baby mama already took his son away when she shacked up with his younger brother and proceeded to also have his brother's son. Both boys now called the non-incarcerated (yet) brother "Daddy," and both were in state custody and my caseload for neglect and abuse.

Big Mama and Alpha Male were just two examples from the 40-some (and ever growing) group of twisted families I was assigned to work with. I coped by practicing to be an alcoholic after work and playing a little game on the way to work: closing my eyes while driving and seeing how high I could count. Think of it as a mini escape-nap so that I could ignore where I was going and what I would have to do when I got there. I quit that social work gig when I got up to nine seconds. I figured there was no point in going to work to help people if there was a good chance I might actually KILL someone while making myself get there.

Besides alcoholism and eyes-shut driving, I've tried out heaps of hobbies to fill up my life with things other than jobs I hated. Music has always been a pleasure for me. There is rarely a moment of the day when I don't have a song playing in my head. I adore watching bands perform and I can air-guitar "Free Bird" as well as anyone in the entire world, so naturally I figured playing an instrument was the perfect pastime to pursue. Like one of those musical geniuses on *America's Got Talent*, I have played the guitar, keyboard, bongos, maracas, and harmonica. And sucked at all of them. Even with lessons. Plus, despite being an excellent singer (in the car, with the radio blasting), my one karaoke attempt sounded more like a cat being strangled than Lady Gaga's "Born This Way." Somehow the music in my head just wouldn't come out my body, so I gave up trying to be musical.

That seems to be the same situation with other leisure activities I've dabbled in. I gave cross-stitch a go, which turned into crap-stitch, which ended up in the garbage. My latch hook "creations" had the same trashy demise. Yoga seemed like a healthy diversion – giving me a nice calming effect, similar to alcohol, but without the requisite hangover and liver damage – but I quit that because I either fell over or fell asleep every time I tried it.

A couple of years ago skateboarding became my "thang." DMan helped me buy a board on eBay, and she was a beauty in hot pink, even her wheels. I named her Pinkie and blinged up her underside with glittery "Hottie!" and "I may not be perfect, but parts of me are incredible" stickers. (The stickers were gifts from my best friend and DMan, so it wasn't really like I was lying about myself!) Oh, the freedom of flying down the street on Pinkie, arms stretched out like wings, hair (and ears) billowing in the breeze. Sheer heaven! That is until I hit a rock and nearly splatted my face on the pavement. Then sheer fear took over. Plus, I never could get the hang of making turns. How embarrassing it was to stop, get off the board, and physically turn Pinkie around every time I came to a corner or wanted to change direction.

In my defense, I stuck with Pinkie for over two years, longer than any of my other wannabe whims. We parted company when every time I jumped on her my mind screamed out: *Roni, you are middle-aged, have no health insurance, and you could literally break your neck and bankrupt yourself with one fall. Get off this hot pink deathtrap!* That took all the fun right out of flying.

So now I'm back to the pursuit of alcohol as a pastime. Actually, I never really left it, but I have refined my repertoire to mostly red wine these days. According to research, it is medicinal and chock-full of flavonoids and resveratrol, whatever the hell those are. And it goes fabulously with my new hobby: Fashion. A glass of Pinot Noir is perfect for watching *Fashion Police*. A zesty Malbec makes a great mate for the *Million Dollar Shoppers* show. And any kind of red pairs well with red-carpet viewing, including Bloody Marys. Hey, it's not wine, but it is red.

Fashion? You may be wondering how someone who claims to be abbie-normal because she is "not truly a chick" gets so into fashion. It was a total fluke because of a different social work job I hated. In order to delay getting to work without employing my eyes-closed driving tactic, I was channel-surfing at home one morning and stumbled onto a show called *Style By Jury*. If you haven't seen the series, they pick one seriously fashion-challenged (and sometimes life-challenged) candidate per episode, put them in front of a secret jury who gives their first impression of the challengee – often with many tears involved in hearing how they truly come across to others – and then give them a makeover in seven days to see what kind of first impression they make before a new jury. We're talking overhauls to hair, makeup, wardrobe, and teeth, with the occasional botox, nip/tuck, and life-coaching thrown in.

I was hooked. Still am when I can find old reruns. Seeing those pitiful Plain Janes transformed into va-va-voom vixens gave me hope – and actual ideas to try – that I could change myself into someone I felt better about being.

For one thing, I have never been feminine. While Mama has a ladylike nose, slender fingers, and dainty hands, I inherited Daddy's schnoz, big-knuckled fingers (yes, I am a knuckle-popper from way back, just like him, which doesn't help), and veiny man-paws. These attributes look fine on him. On me? Not so much. Beyond my physical un-femininity, klutzy should be my middle name. I have knocked my noggin on so many objects that my skull must look like the loser in a demolition derby under my cowlicky hair. My knees are a treasure map of scars from frequent falls, collisions with coffee table corners, and shaving incidents. In fact, my first husband nicknamed me Spike because he said I was so "spike-like." That may have been man-code for "butch," but I let it slide. At least *someone* wanted to marry me.

Then for years I was in a second marriage with lots of love but no sex for a long time. Zilch. FOR YEARS. Let's just say we had issues in the bedroom and leave it at that. Without sex, I sure didn't feel sexy. To his credit, husband #2 thought I looked fine no matter how I dressed, so I mostly bought baggy men's pants and clearance-rack shirts from Walmart because they were comfy. Being barely endowed, I wore quasi-training bras and looked flat as a flitter no matter what I put on. My makeup routine consisted of mascara and moisturizer. Period. The only jewelry you'd see me in was earrings and a watch. Didn't even wear my wedding ring. My style, if you could call it a style, was understated utilitarian un-chic.

My foray into fashion changed all that. Not overnight, mind you, but gradually I expanded my self-vision. Push-up bras replaced training bras as I gave in to the fact that I was never going to look like I had any ta-tas without a bit of padding boosting me in the outward direction. Walmart became reserved only for purchasing groceries and sundries, and I became a savvy shopper for all things funky and fabulous at the Salvation Armani (I stole that name from a book I read. Just couldn't help myself, it sounds so much more refined than Salvation Army Thrift Store!) and finer flea markets. My No Boundaries and Faded Glory labels from Walmart have been replaced by Liz Claiborne, Tommy Hilfiger, Ralph Lauren, even Michael Kors, and all at incredibly low prices. I still don't wear foundation. I figure why waste the money when I look worse WITH it than without it. But, I did replace my decades old CoverGirl Country Woods Collection eye shadow with a bevy of new shadows, blushes, and bronzers to make my eyes sparkle enough to distract from my wrinkles. I hope. And jewelry? Oh hell yeah, I've gone bat-shit crazy for anything bling.

Besides feeling better about myself, I must admit I had an ulterior motive for all the sprucing up: I wanted to get laid! All those years without nookie can make a gal quite randy once her juices get flowing again. And I got laid, exactly what I wanted. Hot, wild, unattached sex. Then I got a boyfriend, exactly NOT what I wanted.

You see, that opens up a whole other chapter on how I am not truly a chick. Most gals want a guy in their life – except lesbians, who want another gal, but it's the same driving force – but not me. The idea of searching for Mr. Right and being saved by Prince Charming? No thanks, I do just fine on my own. I am definitely not the lovey-dovey type. Mushy stuff makes me gag. Cuddle after sex? Um, no. We can share a cigarette, then put your pants on and bye-bye.

Even though I have been married twice, flying solo is much more my M.O. "I wanna do what I wanna do when I wanna do it," as the Trout Fishing in America song goes, suits me to a tee. I just don't "do" relationships well.

But DMan, the boyfriend that I got, didn't care. Every argument I used to convince him that I was lousy at being half of a couple he countered with, "But you ain't never been with me before, Baby." No matter how many times I tried to run him off – for his own good, believe me – he would not be deterred. He puts me to mind of Sheriff Buford T. Justice, a character brought to the big screen bigger than life by Mr. Jackie Gleason, in *Smokey and the Bandit.*

In the movie, Sheriff Justice has been in high-speed pursuit for more than 900 miles trying to apprehend the law-evading Bandit Darville (played by bad boy Burt Reynolds) when smooth-talking Bandit commends the Sheriff on the C.B. radio. "You must be part coon dog, 'cause I've been chased by the best of them, and son, you make 'em look like they're all runnin' in slow motion," Bandit says.

Sheriff Justice replies, "Well, thank you, Mr. Bandit. And as the pursuer, may I say you're the goddamnedest pursuee I've ever pursued. Now that the mutual bullshit it over, WHERE ARE YOU, YOU SOMBITCH?"

Classic movie, nothing but pure mental-vacation with tons of fun-to-quote dialogue. One of my faves.

Sorry to go off on a tangent, but I couldn't throw in the "part coon dog" lines without the Sheriff's comeback. That would be like ordering a Diablo sandwich without a Dr. Pepper – just wouldn't be right. (If you've seen the movie, you get this. If you haven't, you should, then you would.)

Back to DMan. He kept pursuing me, just like Sheriff Justice did The Bandit, and wore me down. He was so sweet despite my bitchiness, so persistent despite my objections. His stick-to-it-iveness offset my fickleness. Somehow he even found my circus-freak combo of elephant ears, big beak, he-man hands, and barely-there boobs to be sexy. Eventually I figured if he can love the hot mess that I am, how can I not love him back?

So I did, and here we are nearly five years later and still together. We survived my crazy McCray-cray spell when I hit age 49 and ran away to live at the beach and be a writer. (I lasted five fabulous beachy months before my money ran out and wrote a book about it, *Life Gone South*, if you are interested in knowing more.) And DMan doesn't seem to mind being the "chick" in our coupledom – crying over reunion stories on the news, especially if a soldier is involved; remembering what we did and even what he wore on special "us" occasions; making up cutesy nicknames and mushy sayings; being the romantic giver of cards and gifts just because – as long as I'm the one that puts on the lingerie as a prelude to sex. I am cool with that too. It gives me another reason to go shopping. (FYI, sometimes the Salvation Armani has some mighty swanky nighties, just make sure to give them a good scalding before you slip them on!) And the sex is still hot and wild, even if it isn't unattached.

So here I am, now 50-something, in a stable relationship with the sweetest man in the entire world who thinks I am "it." (Maybe DMan should be tested?!) I have been working as a Salon Coordinator at an upscale-ish hair salon for nearly two years now, a pretty long stint for me. The job isn't perfect, but most days I enjoy what I do. As a bonus, I get to watch transformations of our clients – just like on *Style By Jury* – every day, so for now I'm sticking with it. I am still digging fashion, red carpets, and red wine (sans the alcoholism that came with doing social work), and don't see myself forsaking them in the near future. Seems like my fickleness has toned down while my chickness has amped up, right? So you may be questioning about now:

Why does this chick keep dredging up feeling like a freak?

I'll tell you why. To the casual observer, I appear normal. Yet in my gut I know I am still an abbie-normal weirdsmobile. Any minute now I might jump off the crazy cliff and quit my job to join the Peace Corps and see the world – if they even take oldsters like me – or to work as a masseuse at some chi-chi resort in Belize and be a beach bumb. Tomorrow I could toss the makeup, let my hair grow out into a mop of wild frizz and cowlicks, get tribal tat sleeves, learn how to ride a motorcycle and just ride, Baby ride, destination unknown. I can feel the fickle flake and not-a-chick in me simmering under the surface at all times.

The thing that is different now is: I don't feel so bad about being a freak anymore. I no longer care what other people think. "Relish the freakdom" is my new motto. Aging does bring on mean, nasty stuff, but at least it gives me perspective to realize that "what is, is," and fighting against reality is a ridiculous waste of energy better spent on hauling my achy ass out of bed every morning to live my life, my way, to the fullest. Yo-freakin'-lo, Roni! (Yolo stands for "you only live once" in case you, like me, aren't up on the current texting acronyms. I googled it.)

A friend recently sent me a bumper sticker that reads "Not all who WANDER are lost." I say a hearty FOR SHIZZLE to that! I finally realized that my flaky-as-a-bisquit form of fickle and lack-of-chickness are just my way of wandering through this world. Hell, I may even shave my head, let my big ears fly, and get that saying tattooed on my forehead to make my crazy visible to the entire world.

So Mama, *I forgive you for not having me tested*. It would have been a big waste of time and money. No pill or therapy would have made a damn bit of difference anyway. Yes, I am a freak. And crazy. And I am just fine with that.

"O"

My

(Spring 2013)

(My "O" arsenal: CD with Ravel's "Bolero," Mr. Purple Passion,
and my fave Janet Jackson CD that gets my "Throb" on!)

It's a crying shame, literally, that in our society we talk
more freely about menopause than orgasm. Suzanne
Somers has made a fortune on TV and in books telling
women how to survive menopause and become their
sexiest post-menopausal selves, but who is the
spokesperson for achieving orgasm? No one. And why
not? Orgasm is sexy and tons more fun than menopause

to talk about and have. So I'm going to buck society (I said "buck," get your mind out of the gutter!) and speak out about orgasm. Move over Suzanne, you Chiclet-toothed, thigh-mastered, menopausal maven, 'cause I'm a coming. (Again, literally.)

Speaking of coming, first let's clarify two terms:

come = to experience orgasm; other tenses include comes, coming, came.
cum = substance ejaculated during orgasm by a male or female. (Yes, females can ejaculate. I heard about it on *Sex And The City*, when Samantha briefly became a lesbian, so it must be true.)

These two words have always confused me, so I did some research to get them right. Thanks to thefreedictionary.com for clarification. And, you're welcome readers, just in case you were confused too.

Second, I am no orgasm expert. Until a couple of years ago, my knowledge of what an orgasm was like came from the deli scene in the movie *When Harry Met Sally*, and I always figured I wasn't having one like Sally did because I didn't have a table to pound on. But I kept trying, and after much experimentation (aka masturbation – hey, I didn't even own a vibrator until I was 48, so I had A LOT of catching up to do), I realized you don't need a table. But, other equipment is certainly a plus.

To make the process simpler for you, here is all that is needed for a do-it-yourself orgasm-achieving starter kit:

TOYS: I've tried the by-hand method many times but I get too bored and tired before I achieve my goal. So toys are a must. In my current arsenal, the Vibrating Bumpy Bullet by Nasstoys is my "uptown" toy, geographically speaking. I think of the Bullet as an appetizer, a delicious tidbit of titillation to whet my orgasm appetite. The nubby texture warms quickly and feels cushiony. You don't want anything abrasive or cold on such a delicate area. She has four speeds – I call it a "she" because only an instrument of the female persuasion could understand what it takes to make me feel *that* good – and she's purple. Perfect because purple is my fave color, especially when it comes to passion. For ease of use, the Bullet has a long cord that attaches to the battery/speed-control box, which adds an element of tingly surprise when you let her dangle. You never know what area her vibration will stimulate next. Besides being arousing fun for you when alone, this toy is also good for use with a partner and *on* your partner. Try it; you'll see.

For my "downtown" pleasure, the Dream Maker by Evolved is just the ticket. It would take a lengthy booklet with diagrams to explain all that Dream does, but the quickie version is: there is a vibrating finger that takes over Bullet's uptown duties while the seven-inch long shaft, the main course for an orgasmic occasion, rotates and vibrates his slightly curved head straight for my G-spot. Dream comes blinged up with multiple speeds and settings, plus flashing purple lights. And he is passion purple, hence the name Mr. Purple Passion. (Yes, I named this toy a "he." He has a shaft; it just made sense. Besides, I feel extra naughty, like I'm having a threesome, sharing the bed with my "she" Bullet and my "he" Purple Passion!)

If you're leery of playing with toys right off the bat or don't want the expense, you might try something you already have around the house. My gal-pal Amy Farrah Fowler from *Big Bang Theory* suggests that "tension-relieving techniques for ladies" can be achieved using an electric toothbrush when male companionship is unavailable. She calls her toothbrush Gerard. She doesn't give how-to specifics on the show, but I'm sure you can figure it out. I haven't tried the "Gerard" method – I'm a manual toothbrush kind of gal – but I am guessing that soft bristles work the best. There's also an episode of *Sex And The City* where Samantha discusses the pros/cons and various uses of "neck massagers" that can offer an alternative to toys (Season Five, Episode Six). So do some experimenting of your own and be creative.

ACCESSORIES: K-Y Warming Jelly is a self-sexer's best buddy, a velvety smooth substitute for foreplay that makes your toys warm up like a lover. A little dab will do you though. Too much becomes a slippery mess. Or lately I've been using coconut oil, at my gyno's suggestion. It's cheap, and you can get it while buying groceries without having to run into weirdos in the condom aisle at Walmart hunting for K-Y Jelly. Coconut oil does solidify below 76 degrees, but it warms quickly in your hands and won't mess up the sensitive pH in your lady parts. Trust me on this: good lubricants and lighting (see below) become sex necessities as you get older. Also, definitely keep a stockpile of batteries so your toys won't run out of juice while you're still juiced up.

ATMOSPHERE: Setting the right mood is key for getting you in the mood. Make sure the room is warm so you'll be comfortable shedding some clothes. The soft glow of candles adds romance and mystery. And really, doesn't everything just look better in candlelight? Having a glass of wine can be a relaxing touch. Music isn't a must, but it helps to get a rhythm going and keep your mind on the mission at hand and not your shopping list. Some personal musical faves are:

- Ravel's "Bolero" – I got turned on to this song by Bo Derek's character in the movie "*10*," and the music's steady climb in intensity and passion gets my lady parts turned on every time. You only have 15 minutes, 38 seconds until the song's climax, so put the track on repeat in case you need longer for your climax.
- Janet Jackson's "That's The Way Love Goes" – The perfect tune for a slow-stroking, relaxing passion date when you follow the smooth thump of the bassline.

- Janet Jackson's "Throb" – A bump-and-grinding
  good time, complete with dirty talk so you don't
  have to.

Come to think of it, if you're not going "Bolero," most
any Janet CD will do for mood music.

Before I divulge my actual how-tos of orgasm,
you may be wondering why I'm focusing on the DIY
method. While I am blessed to be in an intimate
relationship with DMan, one of the planet's best lovers, I
can't always get off when we are getting it on. I'm not
sure why, but it's certainly not his fault. Maybe my
female aiming-to-please instinct keeps me focused on
him more than on myself. Or, maybe I'm great at multi-
tasking in life but not in the sack. I don't know. What I
do know is that when I am alone and follow the soon-to-
come formula, I can achieve orgasm – and not only
orgasm but *yowzagasm*, when my toes curl under, my
back arches, and I involuntarily howl "Yowza!" –
practically every time. That's what I'm hoping for my
readers as well.

I'll share a little-known secret before we jump in
bed (or in the tub or on the couch, your choice) with our
toys or toothbrushes: a true orgasm, especially the
ultimate yowzagasm, can be shy and elusive. For most

women, it doesn't just burst out at the slightest touch like it seems to in the movies. An orgasm must be finessed and nurtured along, like a delicious but delicate dessert soufflé. You must be fully present throughout the "cooking" process and attentive to whether she (your orgasm) needs a little more or a little less heat and time, then tweak accordingly. What works one time may not raise your soufflé the next. So these are merely cooking tips and not foolproof rules.

Now for the how-to, the fun part. The bedroom is warm, the candles flicker, and "Bolero" begins soft and slow. With a pillow propped behind me against the headboard, I recline, knees slightly bent, and press Bumpy Bullet into service. She makes her first contact uptown with a gentle jolt. I gasp. I always gasp, somehow forgetting between pleasure dates how damn good it feels. Then I make her wander, circling around uptown, hitting the downtown hot spots, and vibrating everywhere in between. Some people may enjoy a "backdoor" visit from the Bullet, so try it if you like, but that isn't a big turn-on for me. Then when I'm ready for a change, I dangle Bullet like a pendulum and let her swing where she may, emitting new gasps with each tingling touchdown. Flexing my Kegel muscles in rhythm with her swing heightens the sensation.

The Bullet dance goes on for two minutes, maybe ten. I never watch the clock. I know I'm ready to change partners when I'm excited but wanting more. Time for Mr. Purple Passion to take over.

Nestling the Bullet between my legs, so there's no break in stimulation, I slick up the Dream Maker with my lubricant of choice for the evening. With a click, he whirs into action – purple lights blinking, finger vibrating, shaft rotating – and Bullet steps aside. The finger starts uptown, the tip gently probing my mound with a more targeted quiver than the Bullet can. There's no rush here, so play around with your toy. Get to know what gets you going. From dedicated practice, I've figured out the right side of uptown is particularly fond of attention, so I let the finger linger there. Often. But I've also learned that doing the same thing for too long causes overstimulation, the same as when you walk into a restaurant and salivate at the garlic and parmesan aromas of the alfredo sauce but then can't smell a thing by the time you are ready to order. If you keep mixing up your motions here, you'll keep salivating until dessert is ready.

By now, I'm hungry for the main course. While

the finger continues its uptown shimmy, I slide the Dream Maker's shaft inside for some downtown action. Just a little slide, just an introduction. Oh, yeah. I let out another gasp as the shaft rotates and vibrates, while the finger tingles and teases. After a while, a tinge of euphoria, similar to that feeling at the end of a much-needed and satisfying pee, hits me deep and low inside – my orgasm's calling card. There is a buffet of ways to enjoy the main course and keep the orgasm building: I can let Dream choose the menu by flicking the buttons to different speeds and directions, or I can try a bit of this and a tad of that by moving Dream in circles or figure eights, barely-there thrusts or deeper probes.

I read in a sex book that the majority of our super-sensitive nerve endings are in the outer third of the vagina, and from experience I can attest that it's true. You don't need the shaft-submersing pound, pound, pounding portrayed as orgasmic sex in porn flicks to get the desired effect. That probably gets guys off way more than us gals. Use a light touch and continue experimenting – bet you never knew science could feel so good, huh?! – until you find what feels best for your body on that particular pleasure date.

After partaking in all the delectable options on

the buffet, I know dessert is "coming" when those tinges of euphoria become waves, ripples of titillating tingles that build to a steady pulse from deep inside. I continue with whatever manueuver is satisfying me at the time – usually the barely-there thrusts – fully focused on each sensation, until my vaginal volcano of nerve endings finally explodes in a seismic shiver and I get my yowza-howling, back-arching, toe-curling climax.

Dessert is served. And oh my orgasm, is it delicious!

In the movie, Meg Ryan's character Sally calmly finishes eating her sandwich after her faux orgasm. Me? I lie there as long as I can and relish the bliss. The sex book I read also said that the mind shuts down during orgasm. Damn skippy it does, and those few moments of mindlessness are almost as good as the orgasm. Almost. It's like being in a wide-awake sleep state when my body feels the best it ever feels. EVER. No stress. No pain. No one else to accommodate. Just me, in naked nirvana.

Eventually I finish my wine, get dressed, clean up my toys (proper toy maintenance is also a must!), and head outside for an after-dessert smoke before I rejoin the world. You can devise your own post-orgasm rituals.

But whatever you do, PLEASE, promise me this: Bask in the bliss while it lasts. If you've made the time and effort to give yourself this gift of pleasure all your own, stop and enjoy it. Surviving menopause, writing up that grocery list, or answering work emails can wait.

So that's how I achieve orgasm. It took a lot of years of trial and error and overcoming orgasm myths to find mine, but I'm so glad I did. Feel free to use my recipe or figure out your own, doesn't matter, but have FUN with the journey. There, the orgasm spokeswoman has had her say. I feel better now. Almost orgasmic! Almost.

Wishing you many blissful yowzagasms to come!

Rebel

Holler

(early Winter 2015)

Where have all the rebels gone? History is full of them, folks that marched to the beat of their own drum and banged that thing LOUD:

Patrick Henry - "Give me liberty, or give me death!"

Coco Chanel - "The most courageous act is still to think for yourself. Aloud."

Malcolm X - "I believe in a religion that believes in freedom. Any time I have to accept a religion that won't let me fight a battle for my people, I say to hell with that religion."

James Dean - "Dream as if you'll live forever. Live as if you'll die today."

Che Guevara - "We cannot be sure of having something to live for unless we are willing to die for it."

Gloria Steinem - "A woman without a man is like a fish without a bicycle."

Now those were rebels in the truest sense of the

word: nonconformists, dissenters, agitators, individualists. Major shit disturbers.

Who is in the forefront when you hear about rebels these days? Johnny Depp and Miley Cyrus. While Depp appears rebellious on-screen and off – loved him as Roux in the movie *Chocolat*, what a hottie! – sometimes he is just plain weird. Makes me wonder if he is more please-pass-the-psychotropic-meds wacko than real rebel.

And Miley Cyrus? Puh-lease. Sticking her tongue out perv-style and dressing in outfits from the cheap-hooker cast-offs store does not a rebel make. We already know your Disney days are long gone, Miley, so give up the rebel act, keep your mouth closed, and put on some clothes. Thank you.

I have been a bona fide rebel all my life. One of my proudest memories was from age ten when Daddy was imposing his will upon me yet again and I snapped. He was yelling at me about something I had to do – to this day I hate "have-tos" – and I yelled, "You go to hell," right back at him. Being the daughter of a drill sergeant that had the temper of the Tasmanian Devil was never fun, but it was especially un-fun when I mouthed off while he was still in uniform and wearing his double-grommet web belt. Ouch! He chased me around the yard in full view of the neighborhood, giving me a stinging whack with that belt every time he caught me. Despite the whooping, I was proud that I spoke my mind and bonus proud that I didn't start bawling until after I was alone in my room, exiled to "think about what I had done." No way was I giving Daddy the satisfaction of making me cry.

Since then Daddy and I have formed a truce: He doesn't tell me what to do, and I don't tell him to go to hell. It's a good thing, too, because there is a buttload of bigger things than Daddy to rebel against these days. I may come across like a 95-year old crone bitching about the sad state of the world through clicking dentures because my Poligrip failed, but I don't care. There is a lot of shit going on that I am disturbed about.

Technology

Take technology, for starters. I am a huge fan of the DVR (sorry advertisers, but I kiss your commercials bye-bye every chance I get), Google (makes writing research so much easier), and the digital camera (saves me from blowing cash developing crappy photos since I am The Queen of the what-*IS*-that blurry shots), but most other technologies fall under the category of "just because you can, doesn't mean you should."

Smart phones are a huge pet peeve of mine. Most folks have a stronger bond with their phone than with their significant other. Every time I go to a restaurant I see couples ignoring each other while they check in on Facebook, text with friends, and troll the internet through the entire meal. Ever heard of dinner conversation, you morons? Makes no sense wasting time and money eating out together when you can stay home and play on your phones.

All day long at the hair salon where I work, there is a cacophony of cricket chirps, whistles, bongs, and snippets of songs going off to notify clients (and some of our stylists as well) of urgent texts like "OMG, did U C this? LMFAO!" and life-altering new Instagrams from Taylor Swift and the Kardashians. I am amazed that any hair gets done at all with the constant interruptions. And I can't tell you how many times clients miss their appointments or show up at the wrong time/day because they put in in their phone calendar wrong. What pisses me off even more is how much time is wasted actually loading the information into their damn phone:

click, swipe; click, click, swipe; click, click, click . . .
"Now when is my appointment again?" I talk myself out
of killing them because I would not look good in an
orange prison jumpsuit, then I smile with gritted teeth
and hand them an appointment reminder card.

The other day a client laid her brand new phone
on the counter with a loud, proud thunk, then proceeded
to demonstrate all the "cool stuff" (her words, not mine)
it could do. It was the biggest phone I had ever seen, as
big as my foot and I wear a size nine shoe. After
sufficient oohing and ahhing over the gizmo, I asked,
"Doesn't that get heavy to hold when you're on the
phone?" She replied, "Oh, I don't use it as a phone. I
never talk on the phone anyway."

Huh, so going out to dinner isn't about sharing
conversation and phones aren't for talking anymore?
Interesting. More like hot messed up.

There is even a mental health issue associated
with being so wack-in-love with your phone called
nomophobia. Seriously, it is the "fear of being out of
mobile phone contact" according to Wikipedia. While not
recognized in the DSM-V (Diagnostic and Statistical
Manual of Mental Disorders) yet, it probably will be
soon. So here's a tip for you smart-phone-aholics out

there: You may want to put down or better yet turn off your damn device once in a while before you have to see a shrink and take a Xanax just to get through five minutes without being "connected."

Yes, I do have a cell phone. In fact, I recently had to upgrade because my old 2G (whatever the hell that means) flip phone was no longer going to be serviced by my carrier. Sounded like a scam to make me buy a new phone, but nonetheless I now have a sleek(er) 3G flip phone that actually has a camera. It sucks. The camera is worthless because the pictures turn out even blurrier than my usual snaps, plus I can't download them anyway without spending $20 more on a stupid USB cord. Screw that. And, the ringtone options are lousy, either sounding like someone's-gonna-get-whacked music from a horror flick, which jangles my nerves, or tunes straight out of an AT&T commercial. *I fast-forward through your annoying ads on my DVR, AT&T, why would I want to hear your stupid ad song on my phone?!* And the fucuckta phone won't do a simple task like light up the cover display when I've missed a call the way my antiquated phone did, yet all the complicated functions I don't even use suck the battery down so much that I have to charge it every day.

Upgrade? Yeah, right. The only upgrade was to AT&T's already fat bank account.

Because I paid for it, I'll use the thing. I don't text, email, Facebook, Instagram, Twitter, Pinterest, or Snapchat on it, so I'll muddle through with my dumb phone until the next mandatory "upgrade." I only need it for phone calls anyway and, truthfully, I don't even like those.

Take yesterday, for instance. All I wanted to do was call the pharmacy for a refill on my allergy meds. Should be simple, right? Um, no. By the time I was finished, the entire phone screen was filled up with numbers and symbols from punching this for that, and my back was killing me from sitting on the bathroom floor digging in the medicine box to find the right prescription codes to enter. Never did get to speak to a human being. I recall my grandpa, who passed on several years back, being so frustrated with using the phone that eventually he made my mama make everything but personal calls for him. Grandpa was one of the sharpest people I ever knew, but by the time he would get through all the automated prompts, the poor man would forget what he was calling for, hang up, then have to start all over again.

I reiterate: Just because you companies *can* go cheap by having recordings do your business for you instead of actual people, doesn't mean you *should*.

Social Media

I can't talk technology without bringing up social media. I used to think it was only kids with ADHD who had to be engaged and entertained every minute of the day. Wrong. Adults are just as bad and with no disorder to blame it on.

Wikipedia lists 206 major active social networking sites. 206! And that only includes the "notable, well-known sites." Sheesh! From aNobii (about books) to Zooppa (an online community for creative talent), you can socialized on the web with any kind of group from anywhere in the world. That many options blows my mind, so I'll just stick to the few I've actually heard of.

Facebook *used* to be useful, even fun. When I was cajoled several years ago into getting on Facebook to track down and communicate with high school classmates in planning a reunion, my initial reluctance (aka repugnance) caved in after I started connecting with people I didn't know well in school and got reconnected with friends I'd lost touch with. Posts back then were about personal stuff: who was getting married, divorced, or remarried (sometimes all to the same person, we came from a SMALL town); anecdotes about their kids (and yikes, even grandkids – that made me feel ancient!), cats, and dogs doing amusing things; celebrations, dilemmas, and dramas in our day-to-day lives; and sadly, occasionally, even news of someone we knew that died. That part wasn't so fun, but the rest was like an ongoing, online slumber party that included as many friends as I could "friend" because they didn't all have to fit in my bedroom. My world felt bigger, yet cozier somehow, because of Facebook.

But now? Facebook sucks, both time and energy. The posts are all about "yummy" recipes (I don't cook); "must see" viral videos (I don't do viral); bitchy snipes at President Obama (I *do* have "Obama-care" and it recently saved my ass from emergency-surgery bankruptcy, so thank you very much, Mr. President!); pictures of rainbows inscribed with "do this and God will do that" sermonettes (I don't do religion); and advertisements disguised as "Suggested Posts" (yet again, I don't do ads). To find anything personal or original posted these days – other than a gozillion selfies updated to people's profile pictures – I have to scroll, scroll, scroll and can blow off 30 minutes before I even realize it. I also don't dig wasting time. Just this morning I hopped on Facebook for a specific purpose, waded through page after page of crapola, then couldn't remember my reason for logging on in the first place and logged off in a fit of frustration. (Maybe it runs in the family, huh Grandpa?)

So with all my rebel "don'ts" regarding Facebook, why do I still do it? Fear of missing something *real* happening and feeling left out. Sounds needy, I know, but really it's a need to be needed. Sending personalized happy birthday messages and pump-you-up posts to friends having a rough time allows me to use my creative mojo for the greater good. Hey, even rebels have a squishy side sometimes, and I try to be a positive Facebook force.

Not so for everyone. One of my fave writers, Jen Lancaster (of the *Bitter Is The New Black* book dynasty way before *Orange . . .* honed in), has been ripped a new one umpteen times on Facebook for posts intended to be humorous. In her memoir *I Regret Nothing* (funny, oh so funny!), Jen revealed that a follower posted "I hope you die in a fire" in response to Jen's amusing anecdote comparing a winter of ass-deep snow and ice in her hometown of Chicago to the brief skiff of snow that crippled Atlanta. Don't read it if you don't think something is funny, but resorting to death threats? Come on now, Folks, that's just crazy Mccray-cray overkill.

And it's not only being mean to others on Facebook that has become commonplace. People, particularly women, are (de)meaning *themselves*. As reported in reputable fashion magazines (my most common source of news), researchers have documented an epidemic of folks spending hours on social media comparing their bodies and lives to others and finding themselves lacking. Most women I know could use a boost to their self-esteem, not another means to knock themselves down. The world provides plenty of that already. Besides, how many selfies did those others have to take to get that one perfect, effortless, "oh, I just glanced up and how coincidental that the sun illuminated my highlights and the angle was just right to erase my turkey neck" pose for their profile picture? I'm betting they took a bazillion. And how many vacation photos have you seen of someone stuck on the hotel crapper with diarrhea from sucking down too many fajitas and margaritas? Zero. It's all big smiles and hand-holding strolls on a white sand beach. Same vacation, different presentation with a "photoshopped" spin on it.

Celebrities' bodies and lives are even easier and worse to compare ourselves to, and it can happen subliminally. Taylor Swift is photographed leaving the gym beaucoup times wearing perfectly coiffed hair and couture clothes; her mile-high, spray-tanned legs tucked in Louboutins; and people think, "Why don't I look like that after a workout? Or ever?" When asked about it in interviews, Swift says, "Oh, I take a change of clothes and a hairbrush to the gym," or something similarly nonchalant. Uh, how about a change of clothes; a hairbrush; and a makeup, hair, and stylist entourage? How can anyone compare with that?!

Same sitch in the Twittersphere, where everyone tries to one-up each other with fabulous pix and compressed quips. Not only do I *NOT* want to see more glammed-up celeb photos or snaps of *MY* saggy self, but I am a writer, for Pete's sake. Words are my forte. Why would I choose to have to limit myself to 140 of them in order to play the tweeting game? Me no likey limits or have-tos. And what is up with all the # thises and @

thats? When – and more importantly why – did the number/pound sign and former tic-tac-toe game become a "hashtag" that is a pox on anything written anymore? I do not get it.

Pinterest, Snapchat, and Instagram are social media mediums I also don't get. I will admit that I did Pinterest for a while because I was told it was fun. Not. While finding out folks were "following" my "pins" was a bit of a kick at first, continuing to "pin" unoriginal pictures and sayings to my "boards" just to be social became a Pinterest pain in the ass. When I have to learn a whole new language (hence all the quote marks) in order to participate, count me out.

Snapchat, as I understand it, is for posting photos and videos with captions that can be viewed by a list of specific recipients, then the "snap" disappears after a certain time limit. What is the freaking point in going to all that effort to create something that only a few people can see and then fades away like a fart in the wind?

A freshly-graduated teenybopper I work with explained Instagram to me this way: "My ex-boyfriend Instagrammed him with his arm around this skank, an ex-girlfriend of mine, and I was like 'Two can play that

game,' so I texted his best friend to meet me at a
restaurant and then I Instagrammed a picture of us
flirting at the table with his hands like all over me – but
I don't even really like him – to my ex-boyfriend and my
ex responded 'I'm gonna come down there and kick the
shit out of him,' so I guess we're like getting back
together!"

That description, along with Nicki Minaj and the
Kardashians constantly trying to out-naked each other in
order to enhance their "brands," are all I really know
about Instagram. Sounds more like Insta-skank to me,
so, no thanks. I'll pass on the Instagram experience.

In summation, social media is a serious sucker of
time and energy, it surreptitiously tries to sell you
something and shame you, and it can cause your *real*
relationships to suffer. That is decidedly antisocial. And
even though it is possible to drink while engaging in
social media – which makes almost anything more
palatable in my view – I think I'll stick with having a
glass of wine with actual friends and actually *being*
social.

Politics

I have already spouted off plenty about politics in

"The Craziest One of All," so I'll only add a few tidbits about the current crazies.

It is now 2015 and Donald Trump is the new face (and hair, yikes!) of the Republican Party for the 2016 presidential election. For openers, he harangued Mexico for sending us their drug dealers and rapists in a speech announcing his candidacy. Trump's solution was to "build a great, great wall on our southern border and . . . have Mexico pay for that wall." "Mark my words," he said. I would rather erase his words, and his rhetoric has only gotten more asinine since that speech. The USofA has enough problems trying to deal with increasingly complex world issues already; we don't need a power-hungry bully as President whose only job qualifications are buying and selling everything in sight for mega profits and saying, "You're fired."

Currently there are 38 declared Republican Party presidential candidates, so many that there had to be two initial debates held: an early-bird special with the I-don't-know-who-the-hell-that-is candidates, and the prime-time show featuring the ten front-runners. No, I did not watch. First of all, I lean toward the Democrats and I can't even stand to watch their debates. BORING! Second, the debate was on Fox News, which in my opinion causes brain damage. Just speak with someone who watches Fox News exclusively, notice the vacant eyes and the Stepford-style mimicry of everything said on that channel, and you'll see what I mean. Third, I could not stand to watch Trump and his floppy comb-over embarrass himself and our country any more than he already has. So while I cannot speak firsthand about the debate particulars, I can report that "The Donald" Trump is currently at the top of the Republican pack in the polls.

America, we are in some seriously deep shit if this Trump-mania continues.

Now to the Democrats. Obama is out, two terms and done. Nineteen candidates have officially declared they will run, with Hillary Clinton on top of the heap of mostly unknowns. The Republicans are doing all they can to knock her off that heap, currently focusing on missing data from the time she was Secretary of State. The most recent Republican soundbite was a reporter asking whether Clinton's email server had been "wiped clean of data," and Clinton snarkily responding, "What – like with a cloth or something?"

I totally get her answer if she was being snarky because she doesn't like to clean. I abhor cleaning and get snarky about having to do it too. But if that wasn't the reason, then it makes Hillary sound guilty, as if she's covering up something. We've finally had our first black President; now I think it's time for a woman as Pres, so I'm rooting for you, Hill. But for fuck's sake, keep the cover-up in your makeup bag and tell the truth.

Speaking of truth, Vice President Joe Biden is currently testing the waters about running for President. While a likable but tough-as-nails fellow, Biden may be way more *truth* that this country can handle. The dude doesn't have a brain-filter that catches the don't-say-that shit before it flies out of his mouth and hits the fan. Case in point, at the signing of the Affordable Care Act, Biden whispered to President Obama, "This is a big fucking deal," loud enough for reporters to hear and quote. Yeah, Joe, it is a B-F'ing-D, but don't say it out loud!

Huh? This is the best we've got as options for President? Trump, who doesn't care what he says or who he offends; running against Hillary, who puts more spin on her comments than a washing machine; or against Joe no-filter Biden. The 2016 presidential race is going to be a wild ride, that's for sure.

I don't know who will win, but what I do know is

this: If we, the people, did our jobs like most politicians, saying whatever it takes to get the job and then doing whatever the hell we want after we get it, we'd all be unemployed. Come to think of it, it might be fun for The Donald to become President just so we can say "You're fired" when he screws up. And he will. Mark my words.

Religion

I am not religious. Just ask the preacher's wife where my parents used to attend church. I only showed up to hear Mama sing a special number, then tried to make a quick post-sermon getaway when the lady cornered me in the parking lot. With a limp handshake and a sickenly sweet smile, the wife said, "We're so glad you came and we hope you'll come back soon."

"I'm not real religious," I said. "So, no, I won't be back."

With that said, the handshaking stopped. Her eyebrows shot up, while her mouth fell into a shocked "O" followed by a toothless, clenched smile. She dropped my hand as if it was Satan's own, and I skedaddled. Shock value, one of the many joys of being a rebel.

During one of my frustrating Facebook perusals, I did come across this gem of a quote which sums up my view of religion perfectly:

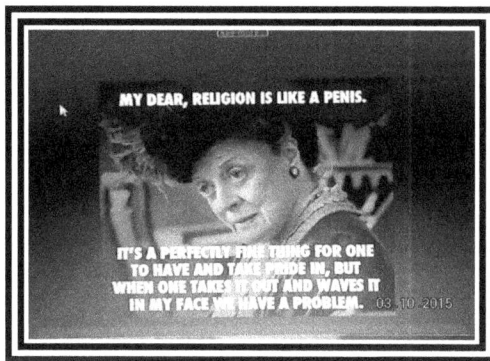

I liked it so much, I snapped a picture of the screen to remember the quote. Through a Google search, I found out that Dowager Countess Violet Crawley, played by Dame Maggie Smith, uttered this delicious dialogue on the series *Downton Abbey*, and it spread like wildfire through social media. Not being an *Abbey* watcher myself, I'm not sure what the Countess's beef is with religion, but I certainly like her style.

What I don't like is that people who *are* real religious replace their brain with the Bible. Maybe it's because I live smack dab in the buckle of the Bible Belt – Missouri is actually more like the nipple if you look at a map of the "belt," but buckle sounds better – but folks around here seem to lose their minds when they get religion. If a preacher or the Bible doesn't say it, then IT can't be true. No matter what the "it" is. Trying to have a discussion about any number of sensitive subjects makes hardcore Christians grip the Good Book tighter than a virgin's thighs on a first date and begin spewing scripture. Trust me on this, as I have attempted tackling these taboo topics in conversation:

- ✔ Why the separation of church and state is necessary in a democracy;
- ✔ Why it is only fair to allow gay couples to marry if they want to suffer the confines of matrimony the same as straight folks (I don't dig marriage any more than I dig religion);
- ✔ How having prayer in school and various other venues (including all of our family get-togethers where eating is involved, with mandatory hand-

holding!) might make non-prayers (yes, ME!) feel
squirmy and violated;

✔ And, why saying "Happy Holidays" instead of
"Merry Christmas" does not mean I am
possessed by the Devil!

Enough already with the preacher quoting and Bible
beating. I can go to church or read the book myself if I
wanted someone else's opinion on our topic of
conversation. I want to know what YOU think. That is if
you could/would think for yourself.

Speaking of opinion, there are umpteen theories
on who wrote the Bible. Google it, you'll see. It appears
that except for those quoting the Bible left and right,
most people don't believe God and/or his emissaries
actually penned the Good Book. I may get smote down
by a lightening bolt for saying this, but my fave
hypothesis is: Once upon a time a bunch of Catholic
muckety-mucks were locked up together to compile a
comingling of religious writings with their own original
edicts, all under the guise of "the word of God," and
when The Church was satisfied that the resulting book
would scare the bejesus out of the church folk and get
them to quit running amok, *The* Bible was born. Since

most of organized religion's role is to control people's behavior, that seems like a perfectly plausible postulate to me.

Nope. No wrathful lightening struck me. I'm still here, so I may as well continue my rebel rant.

Church? No thanks, not for me. I was raised in the Baptist church but quit going after my parents quit making me. Then a long time ago, when I moved to a new state as an adult, I thought it was a good idea to try church again, that maybe I could connect with the community and meet people there. No again. The only thing I connected with was the offering plate passed four times during the service. Yes, FOUR! I never darkened that church door again.

Then my aunt Peg was keen on the Unitarian Church being different, so I checked it out when I moved to Myrtle Beach, South Carolina. The Unity Christ Chapel was different, all right. Perched in a strip mall next door to Patty's Bar – which, inconveniently, wasn't open on Sundays – the Chapel experience was more of a love-in musical than a church service.

A full band, complete with bongos, belted out several sing-along numbers, followed by a mini-sermon all about love and peace from a lady lay-preacher. Next, we meditated on her message "to send our love and peace out into the world." Some folks were even in full lotus position on the pews. Someone sitting near me was rocking so much Patchouli oil that I was expecting them to pass me a doobie instead of the blinged-up coffee can they used for the offering. The finale was the band wailing a churched-up version of Joe Cocker's "Feelin' All Right" as the congregation held hands, sang and swayed to the beat, and group-hugged. Between too much touchy-feely with people I didn't even know and the coffee can coming around a second and third time for more money, I'd had enough. I snuck out and never went back. That was the end of me trying the "church" experience.

Church comes up in conversation a lot where I live. Inevitably people will ask, "Where do you go to church?" With a sweet smile, I reply, "Nowhere. I'm a heathen." Again with the shock value, that shuts them up. Since they don't throw out a church invite or start praying for my soul right there, I'm guessing they think that I'm kidding. Or maybe they think I just haven't found my "church home" yet. I let them think what they want as long as they leave me alone.

But telling people I don't believe in God? This

rebel doesn't holler so much about that.

God is a given, like air and water, for nearly everyone I come in contact with. Therefore in their eyes, not believing in God makes me: a) a witch; b) the Devil; or c) a pitiful lost soul. I can handle being considered a witch, rocking the whole Stevie Nicks "Rhiannon" vibe. That's cool. And I have so many hot flashes these days that it feels like I'm in hell anyway, so being the Devil isn't too far off track. But pity? That "tsk" of sad disapproval with their tongue, the I'll-pray-for-you pat on my shoulder, and the raised eyebrows over "you poor thing" eyes? Um, no, I don't need your pity.

I am not an ignorant heathen from a third-world country who the share-the-Gospel-and-save-a-soul Christians believe needs to be enlightened about God. I know all about God. We go way back. Despite not being religious, I *was* spiritual for a long time and did a lot of praying. Even kept a notebook of those who were ill, dying, unemployed, or just facing some crisis and would benefit from an extra mention in God's ear. I'd had times of doubt before, wondering whether there was a God at all, but I kept on praying anyway. Then came a time when people on the list were dying constantly, when I was depressed and my life was a mess, when nothing I prayed for was getting any better. I thought: *Is God on vacation or what?*

I mentioned this to someone I was close to, that I didn't think God was listening, and they said, "When you ask God for something, his response is either 'Yes, no, or wait.'" WTF?! I could get those same odds without God, without pages of prayer requests and all the time and energy it took to lift them up, and without feeling the undercurrent of judgment that I must be outside God's favor because my prayers weren't answered.

I broke up with God that very day. Haven't missed him/her/it at all. Ours was like those sad one-sided relationships in chick flicks: one person (me) actually *in* the relationship and doing all the work, and the other person (God) sucking up all the attention and never really committing. At least not that I could tell. Only in the movies, once the chick finally gets fed up and dumps the noncommittal dude, he realizes what he lost, busts his ass to woo her and win her back, then they live happily ever after. Not me, not in my story. When I split up with someone, we are D-O-N-E. I am not looking for a fantasy-savior relationship. I'll take care of myself like I always have. Whatever happens, happens. Like it always has, God or no God. Going solo is just fine with me.

Not praying is fine with me as well. Haven't
missed that either. I feel lighter, freer, without the
burden of all those prayer requests ping-ponging
through my brain and dragging me down. The whole
prayer thing brings to mind pictures from the Bible of
Jesus walking through a crowd with folks grabbing at his
robe and begging for healing. If Prozac were around
back then, I'm certain Jesus would have eaten them by
the fistful.

There is an awkwardness about not being a
prayer though. Those few personal posts that still exist
on Facebook usually detail some tragedy or dilemma and
end with "prayers appreciated." When I first quit
praying, I simply ignored the posts and didn't reply. That
felt cold, even for a rebel. So now I click "like" – which
seems even more awkward to "like" a post about
someone that is suffering, but when on Facebook, do as
the Facebookers do – and post some inane but heartfelt
cliché, usually "Hang in there!" or "I'll send positive
energy your way!" I figure if the answer to actual prayer
is "yes, no, or wait," then my responses have just as
much probability of helping.

Despite my having mentioned to her *once* that I

no longer believe in God or prayer, Mama still asks me to pray for folks when we talk on the phone every day. It is a job to her, being a "prayer warrior" as she calls it. She keeps a journal of prayer requests (I stole the idea from her) and frequently makes her rounds by phone to check on the status of the prayees. Rather than repeat myself when she gives me these requests – *Mama, I told you before, I do not pray* – and thus add one more prayer need to her long list, this time for my damned soul, I just say, "Okay, Mama," and let it go. Life is much simpler that way.

Telling Daddy to "Go to hell" at age ten is one thing, but telling Mama to go to hell by blatantly dissing all that she believes in? That is some shit this rebel will not disturb.

(This is what a real rebel looks like Miley, no
perv-tongue required. I do dig the rock
hand sign, though, so I stole it. Thank you!
And yes, Readers, I'm still using the
"upgrade" flip phone. It still sucks.)

The Final

Countdown

(January 2015)

Robin Williams died on August 11, 2014. The world was stunned that this hilarious comedian, who made us laugh (and I'll admit it, sometimes pee my pants a little) from his machine gun-blast style of improv and endless well of wacky personas, would hang himself from his closet door. Even I was stunned, and I think about death all the time.

I was also a tad glad that he did it, put an end to his own despair, especially after learning that he had bouts of deep depression, battled drug and alcohol addiction, and had recently been diagnosed with Parkinson's disease. While Williams' passing was a devastating blow to his family, friends, and fans – and believe me, I had someone I loved commit suicide and I'm not sure that the ones left behind ever get over it – the man deserves kudos for taking control of the one BIG inevitable in life that is normally out of our control.

On the flip side, barely three weeks later, my beloved *Fashion Police* guru Joan Rivers goes in for a "minor throat procedure," stops breathing, and never recovers. Dead, September 4, 2014, at 81 years young. With all of her highly-publicized nips and tucks, Joan looked younger than her daughter Melissa, and she had come back from career death so many times that she seemed immortal. I was flabbergasted.

"I have never wanted to be a day less than I am," Rivers said in 2013. "People say, 'I wish I were 30 again.' Nahhh! I'm very happy HERE. It's great. It gets better and better. And then, of course, we die." A punch line for an interview, Joan, but oh so true.

Death. No matter if we choose it like Robin, or it sneaks up and snatches us like Joan, we are all headed toward death in some form or fashion. Each of us, whether creeping along at fate's pace or barreling at warp speed fueled by disease, is approaching that final countdown. Yeah, I think about it a lot and I don't fear death. Sounds like the ultimate vacation to me: no more worries, done with decisions to make, no more trying to figure things out or get my life "right." I won't mind saying sayonara to stress and striving and welcoming an endless hiatus from rules and have-tos. I look at death as just a peaceful, quiet, infinite black. I may feel differently when the Grim Reaper joins me between the sheets, but I don't think so.

Best of all, there will be no more pain and suffering. That is what scares the bejesus out of me: Suffering.

In the World Series of suffering, I am a bottom-of-the-lineup rookie that hasn't even batted yet. Compared to folks who have faced debilitating disease, terrible tragedy, or life-altering accidents (or heaven forbid, all three!), I have skated through 50-plus years nearly unscathed. I've never had any broken bones, and my first major surgery was just this past year when my appendix shot craps and oozed infection into my abdomen.

I know I've been lucky. The final story on the *Nightly News* is forever chronicling some unfortunate someone who has suffered horribly but rose above their circumstances to cure _____ (insert: obscure disease or phobia), write a prize-winning _____ (insert: memoir, symphony, or Hallmark channel movie), or compete in a _____ (insert: triathlon, pie-eating contest, or *American Idol* spin-off), despite having lost their _____ (insert: an appendage or one of the senses). I make light of their stories, but these news-worthy people persevere in light of some pretty awful plights and don't seem to suffer.

That ain't me.

Everything makes me suffer:

:(Putting on pants every morning is like stuffing my lower half into a sausage casing because I've put on 12 pounds since cutting back on smoking and I refuse to buy bigger clothes. Let's see: I smoke, can't breathe, feel bad about myself, and suffer; or I don't smoke, get fat(ter), feel bad about myself, and suffer. It's a tossup.

:(In the late 1980s, a pickup truck hit me while I was walking, leaving me majorly bunged up. Past suffering. Now since I've hit my 50s – which feels more like my 50s hit me, HARD – my entire body hurts. Whether my aches and pains are residuals from the accident or just a normal part of mid-life, I don't know. What I do know is that a day without ibuprofen is a day when I don't feel like getting out of bed. Present suffering.

:(Unless you are like Harry Burns of *When Harry Met Sally . . .* and are reading this last chapter first in case you die before you finish the book, you know of my ongoing battle with the sags and drags of aging. Looking in the mirror to put on makeup and slathering lotion on my body every morning are constant reminders that I'm losing the war against "the south" (aka my skin is slumping southward and taking everything underneath with it). Suffer. Then this morning, as I am plucking the plethora of white hairs out of my sweaty brows, I miss

the whites and get a mess of browns instead. Now my
brows look like a rapper's head with his name shaved
into his 'do. I think my rapper name reads "Don't." More
suffering. What if the missing hairs all grow back
white?? I love my beautiful mama, but I swear if I have
to start drawing on eyebrows like she does every
morning, I am going to put aside my extreme distate for
that goober Justin Bieber and wear a ski mask whenever
I'm in public like he does, Chanel or not. I cannot even
imagine how much my brows are going to sweat if they
are all painted on and stuck inside a mask. Suffering on
suffering.

:(My life sucks. It is the dead of winter, and I hate
winter as any beach babe (at heart) does. I also hate
my job working at a hair salon. While I survived the
holidays – which is akin to riding out a hurricane EVERY
DAMN DAY from two weeks before Thanksgiving until
after New Year's Day because our clients go all crazy
cakes from needing to get their hair done for every
event and family picture – now I have to hear about all
the fabulous trips to the beach our clients just returned
from or are packing for, and I am stuck here. In
Missouri. In January. In a job I hate, in hopes of winning

the lottery and un-sucking my life. Suffering.

:(The topper this morning was checking my Friday
night Mega Millions ticket to find out that I didn't win,
yet again. Some sumbitch in Illinois won the $270
million that coulda-shoulda been mine. Suffering
succotash, I can't catch a break from suffering.

Don't hate me because I am a big wussy.
Alcoholics are forgiven all the time for admitting they
are powerless when it comes to alcohol. Well, I admit it:
I am powerless when it comes to suffering.

I try, I really do, to put on my big-girl panties in
the face of adversity and be a brave non-whiner. When
things go awry, I often remind myself of one of my
sweetie DMan's favorite sayings: "It's all about mind
over matter. If you don't mind, it doesn't matter."
Unfortunately, when I hear him say this in my head, I
want to smack him because I damn well DO mind when
I suffer, so it DOES matter.

In my defense, I am not a selfish sufferer. When
anyone suffers, I suffer. So many people I know are
dealing with cancer and all that implies: chemo,
radiation, hair loss, removals, reconstructions . . . the

list of horrors goes on and on. The "Big C" certainly seems to have metastasized throughout our society, hasn't it? And with each battle against cancer that I hear about or witness, I don't just empathize. Nooooo. I feel it viscerally, like a pointy-toed boot plowing into my gut.

And it's not just people. Dogs in distress? I am a mess! Even seeing a dog – or any animal – being rescued from raging flood waters half a world away on the news makes me a basket case for the rest of the day. A client told me yesterday about having to put her dog down (the poor dog was already 15 years old and had lymphoma and leukemia, so it really was for the best), and both of us ended up in tears. After work, I mailed her a condolence card.

The dictionary.com definition of "suffer" reads "to undergo or feel pain or distress." That is the crux of my suffering situation. While I may not actually be *undergoing* what other folks consider pain or distress, it sure as shit FEELS like it to me.

This isn't my fault. My SOS (suffering oversensitivity – I coined the term myself) is genetic. Not only did I inherit Daddy's protruding proboscis and fat-knuckled man hands, I also inherited his woe-is-me way of life. While Mama is Miss Mary Sunshine and convinced that prayer can cure anyone of anything, Daddy has Chicken Little's the-sky-is-falling view of everything. The man endured Vietnam, being an Army drill sergeant in a special training company of fuck-ups, and 20-plus years working for the postal service for Chrissakes, but let him get a sniffle or see the price of gas go up more than ten cents in a day and he carries on like the world is coming to an end. Which leads us – meaning anyone who is around him for any length of time – to wish it *were* coming to an end to put an end to his incessant whining. And I, thanks to one more generous genetic gift from Daddy, am the same damn way.

So you see, not only will death be the ultimate vacation from suffering for me, but the world will suffer less when I am gone from having one less whiner in it. Double bonus! From that viewpoint, my pro-death stance is downright altruistic instead of morbid. Maybe I do have some of Mama's Mary Sunshine in me after all. But when it *is* my time, I just hope that death takes me quick, because if I have to suffer . . . .

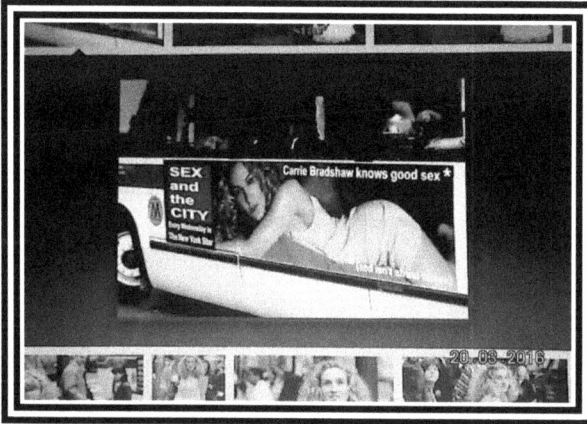

(My top quick-death picks are:
1) a whopper of a one-and-done heart attack,
or 2) this big-ass bus hitting me head on.
Hey, if I can't BE Carrie Bradshaw,
getting hit by a bus with her
on it is the next best thing!
And maybe *Sex And The City 3* can be
about the gals reuniting for their
biggest fangirl's funeral? I'd better quit thinking
about death and get to work on the screenplay!)

ACKNOWLEDGMENTS

Thank you, Readers, for giving me a bit of your valuable time and attention. I hope I made it worth the effort!

Thanks to my Sweetie, DMan, for putting up with me, because life sure can be crazy living with me, especially when I am in writer mode. You're the best, Doodle!

A special shout-out to Sister K for being in my book and being so much wicked cool fun to hang out with.

To my friend Sparkle: You know I love you more than my luggage! I couldn't have finished this book without your encouragement and unwavering belief in me as a writer.

Lastly, thanks to Mama for *not* reading this book. (If you did, sorry if I disappointed you. This is just me being me. If I can't write my truth, I won't write at all. And, I will buy you a new white-out pen to replace the one you probably used up to cover all the bad words!)

ABOUT THE AUTHOR

Roni Blanche lives in Missouri with her life buddy DMan, who recently "upgraded" her old flip phone to a smart phone as a birthday gift. She still can't figure out how to operate the phone most of the time, and her fat-fingered, man-paws are always hitting the wrong keys. So if you get an undecipherable text, it is probably from her. She has written two previous books, *Life Gone South (when I ran away to live at the beach and be a writer)* and *Life Is A Beach – After I'm Gone*, both available on Amazon.com. You can catch her latest reality writing at lifebecrrr-azy.blogspot.com, rantsandravesbyroni. blogspot.com, and adventuristaroni.blogspot.com., or you can read her book reviews at bookcrrr-azygal.blogspot.com.

www.ingramcontent.com/pod-product-compliance
Lightning Source LLC
Chambersburg PA
CBHW060753050426
42449CB00008B/1384